DON'T Teach the Canaries NOT to Sing

*To Alene Christiano, who has shown generations of
educators "how to do school."*

DON'T Teach the Canaries NOT to Sing

Creating a School Culture That Boosts Achievement

Robert D. Ramsey

A Joint Publication

CORWIN PRESS
A SAGE Publications Company
Thousand Oaks, CA 91320

NATIONAL ASSOCIATION
OF SECONDARY SCHOOL
PRINCIPALS
promoting excellence in middle and high school leadership

For information:

Corwin Press
A Sage Publications Company
2455 Teller Road
Thousand Oaks, California 91320
www.corwinpress.com

Sage Publications India Pvt. Ltd.
B 1/I 1 Mohan Cooperative Industrial Area
Mathura Road, New Delhi 110 044
India

Sage Publications Ltd.
1 Oliver's Yard
55 City Road
London EC1Y 1SP
United Kingdom

Sage Publications Asia-Pacific Pte. Ltd.
33 Pekin Street #02–01
Far East Square
Singapore 048763

Printed in the United States of America

Library of Congress Cataloging-in-Publication Data

Ramsey, Robert D.
Don't teach the canaries not to sing: Creating a school culture that boosts achievement/ Robert D. Ramsey; A joint publication with the National Association for Secondary School Principals.
    p. cm.
Includes index.
ISBN 978-1-4129-4893-7 (cloth)
ISBN 978-1-4129-4894-4 (pbk.)
    1. School environment. 2. Academic achievement. 3. School management and organization. I. Title.

LC210.R36 2008
371.2—dc22   2007014592

This book is printed on acid-free paper.

07   08   09   10   11   10 9 8 7 6 5 4 3 2 1

Acquisitions Editor:	Elizabeth Brenkus
Editorial Assistants:	Desirée Enayati and Ena Rosen
Production Editor:	Melanie Birdsall
Copy Editor:	Bill Bowers
Typesetter:	C&M Digitals (P) Ltd.
Proofreader:	Cheryl Rivard
Indexer:	Holly Day
Cover Designer:	Scott Van Atta

Contents

Preface

Why This Title

D r. Alene Christiano is a lifelong educator from California. I've never met her, but I know her by correspondence, her reputation, her work, and her writing. Alene has been a successful teacher and teacher of teachers well into her eighties. Over her extended career, she has developed (and generously shared) a series of practical precepts for professionals on "how to do school." My favorite is "Don't teach the canaries not to sing."

All licensed physicians take the Hippocratic Oath, part of which is to do no harm to the patient. If you believe Alene Christiano's teachings, educators should be required to take a similar solemn oath. All educators need to assure that no school practice, protocol, or policy inhibits or stifles student creativity and learning. Nothing in or about the school should "teach the canaries not to sing." Unfortunately, this is not always the case today.

Most children enter school eager-eyed, excited about learning, and anxious to learn. Their parents are excited too. But by high school, many of these same students and parents become alienated and disengaged from the school. Some are lost for good.

Something in the culture of many schools turns kids off, burns out staff members, distances parents, and cools community support. Something is causing too many students and families to lose interest, lose hope, and lose out. Christiano thinks this is unacceptable. So do I.

Our schools should help students—and all stakeholders—find their voices, instead of teaching the canaries not to sing. That's why I chose this title. And that's what this book is about. Thank you, Alene.

Acknowledgments

All writers rise on the backs of others. Acknowledgments, then, are the primary currency for paying back debts of gratitude. Without acknowledgments, the writer writes under false pretenses and is both an ingrate and a counterfeit.

That's why I want to acknowledge all those who contributed to the completion of this work. First, my greatest gratitude must go to the seven superintendents, dozens of principals, and countless teachers in three award-winning school districts who have allowed me into their remarkable school cultures over the course of my career. They taught me about school cultures from the inside out.

Second, and more specifically, I am also deeply indebted to Robb Clouse, Editorial Director at Corwin Press, who challenged me to write this book; Lizzie Brenkus, Corwin Press's Acquisitions Editor, who always makes me feel up to the challenge; the entire corps of editors and assistants at Corwin Press (especially Melanie Birdsall and Bill Bowers), who helped make the challenge achievable; and, of course, to my unbeatable wife, Joyce, who always walks with me and works with me throughout the entire creative journey. Thanks to all of you!

PUBLISHER'S ACKNOWLEDGMENTS

Corwin Press gratefully acknowledges the contributions of the following individuals:

Frank Buck, Curriculum Supervisor
Talladega City Schools
Talladega, AL

Virginia Drouin, Principal
Alfred Elementary School
Alfred, ME

Cary Dritz, Associate
    Superintendent
Ventura County Office of Education
Thousand Oaks, CA

Edward Drugo, Principal
Latrobe Elementary School
Latrobe, PA

David N. Fischer, Superintendent
Oswego City School District
Oswego, NY

Robert W. Fowls, Head of School
Trinity Lutheran School
Bend, OR

Harriet Gould, Principal
Raymond Central
   Elementary School
Valparaiso, NE

Stephen Handley, Superintendent
Hinds County School District
Raymond, MS

Lawrence Kohn, Principal
Atascocita High School
Humble, TX

About the Author

Robert D. Ramsey is a lifelong educator with extensive frontline experience as a proven leader of leaders in three award-winning school districts in two different states. Most recently, he served as Associate Superintendent in St. Louis Park, Minnesota, which has been named one of the Top 100 Communities for Youth in the nation, and where every elementary and secondary school has been recognized by the federal government as a Blue Ribbon National School of Excellence.

Ramsey is also the author of several successful professional books, including the bestselling *Lead, Follow, or Get Out of the Way,* and is a frequent contributor to numerous popular journals and newspapers. Ramsey's other Corwin Press books include *School Leadership From A to Z, What Matters Most for School Leaders,* and *Inspirational Quotes, Notes, & Anecdotes That Honor Teachers and Teaching.*

Currently, Ramsey works full-time as a freelance writer in Minneapolis with his wife, Joyce, where they are close to their two grown children and four grandchildren.

Introduction

Culture Shock

We have it in our power to begin the world again.

—Thomas Paine, author of *Common Sense* (1776)

My widowed mother died when I was a 16-year-old sophomore in high school. I had to move away to live with my older sister in another (and much larger) city. I was uprooted from a small community of 2,000 residents where I knew everyone and was replanted in an urban high school of 2,000 students where I knew no one. In midyear. With little or no preparation. That's culture shock!

I felt lost and overwhelmed. I didn't know how to fit in. I didn't know the unwritten rules and roles, the insider jokes, the code words, or the secret handshake. I didn't know the history, the traditions, the stories, the heroes, the values, the taboos, or the boundaries. I soon learned that the pecking order of the culture relegated newcomers to a marginal role in the life of the school.

My grades suffered. My confidence and fragile teenage psyche suffered. I suffered. I felt like an outsider—disconnected and invisible. The culture seemed impenetrable. It wasn't at all welcoming, accepting, supportive, or empowering for me. It took a full year and a half for me to begin to get back on track and to reclaim my voice and my place at the fire.

But by all commonly accepted measures and standards, this was not a bad school. It had a rich history, a good reputation, distinguished alumni, fine facilities (including a bell tower and even a mast from the historic U.S.S. *Constitution,* known as "Old Ironsides"), prestigious faculty, and a world-class curriculum. But it didn't work for me.

For a vulnerable teenager, the culture of the organization was a much greater influence than its image, buildings, programs, or faculty credentials. That's the way it is in schools—and in most human institutions. It's not the edifices or external trappings that matter most. It's the unseen, unpublicized, and undocumented culture of the organization that really makes all the difference.

Of course, my unfortunate experience in high school wasn't all that unique. It is potentially repeated (in varying forms and degrees of intensity) every time a child enters a new class, changes schools, or moves to the next-higher level. And it's not just newcomers who are affected (positively or negatively) by cultural imperatives, expectations, standards, and demands. Everyone is.

More than any other single factor or influence, the organizational culture promotes, allows, or limits individual and group performance and success. In most schools, kids make it—or don't—largely because of the existing culture. Not just the new kids. But all kids. And adults, too.

Culture counts! In every school—in your school—how people relate, interact, communicate, talk to each other, talk about each other, and solve problems together (or not) is a significantly greater determiner of success than class size, what courses are taught, what books are used, or how much money is spent. The best school leaders in the business understand this and consciously do something about it. You should, too.

Want a better school? Better-trained teachers can help. So can spiffed-up facilities. And so can more up-to-date curriculum and materials. Adding more tests may also help some. But improving relationships and the overall culture of the school will help most of all.

Bad schools have toxic cultures that work against pupil learning, teacher effectiveness, parent involvement, and community support. Contrarily, good schools have healthy, supportive, affirming, and liberating cultures that work for everyone—even the shy new kid on the block.

Good or bad, school cultures are organic. They grow and change. Leaders can change them. Effective administrators do it all the time. And best of all, it doesn't cost any more to create a healthy culture than to create an unhealthy one.

Unfortunately, many school officials don't know much about the culture of their own school or pay much attention to the sociology of the organization. They just let the culture "happen." It's a huge mistake and, sometimes, a fatal one.

In administrator school, prospective and practicing principals and superintendents learn a great deal about school law, finance, budgeting, contract negotiations, tests and measurements, statistics, scheduling, pupil transportation, curriculum development, learning theory, child psychology, and much more. Whew!

They usually don't, however, learn very much about how to create a positive school culture. In fact, it seems that *avoiding* this topic is part of the culture in some graduate schools.

So culture building is often the one "must-learn" subject that no one ever teaches you anything about. It's also the one major reform the reformers most often forget.

Naturally, there are other ways to learn about shaping school cultures than going to school. Painful experience and trial and error might work. But at what cost? A much easier and simpler way is to tap into existing knowledge and the wisdom and experience of other successful school leaders, past and present. That's where this little book comes in.

Don't Teach the Canaries Not to Sing is a primer on the invisible curriculum—the organizational culture that determines what kind of place the school really is. Not intended as a research report, this guide draws on a broad spectrum of experiential and anecdotal material to give busy readers practical, day-in and day-out tips for making the school a better place to teach and learn. Through concrete real-world examples, insider insights, and down-to-earth explanations, the following pages demystify the phenomenon of school culture. Without resorting to lofty (and unintelligible) jargon or obtuse psychobabble, the text clearly defines what the culture of a school is, where it comes from, how it works, and why it is critically important.

More significant, each chapter is packed with the specific information, guidelines, skills, strategies, initiatives, and techniques needed—as well as the warning signs and pitfalls to avoid—to create a school culture that works for everyone and makes possible peak performances by students and teachers, along with maximum support from parents and community members.

A school isn't just a building. Or a bunch of books. Or whatever it says in the parent handbook. It is a complex web of relationships, rules, roles, and rewards that make up the real teaching and learning environment.

Effective school leaders strive to shape this environment to benefit all stakeholders. You don't want to do any less for your school. That's reason enough to read on.

Best of all, this no-nonsense little book can become the user's manual on school cultures that you can't get elsewhere. Reading it will force you to look at your organization in a different way—and, just maybe, to really see it for the very first time. Can you afford not to take a look?

1

School Culture Under the Microscope

What It Is, How It Works, and Why It's So Important

School is a state of mind.

—John Gardner, founder of Common Cause

———————— ❧ ————————

I t's more important to student success than the curriculum. The reading program. The basic texts. Technology. The physical plant. Or even the testing program. And it's more important to teacher morale and effectiveness than wages, benefits, or working conditions. What is it? It's the culture of the organization.

No, we're not talking about the school's art and music program or about some glob of microplasm that pupils examine under a microscope in a school science lab somewhere. We're talking about the core values, cherished beliefs, ingrained expectations, norms of behavior, and the unwritten rules, roles, and rituals that make up the context in which everyday teaching and learning take place.

Sound a little too "fuzzy," soft, vague, or ethereal to be of interest to practical-minded, overburdened, hard-scrapping, hard-scrambling, every-day school administrators? It shouldn't. These factors are the true driving forces in the rough-and-tumble real world of what we call school. Together, they constitute the organizational culture that defines what kind of place the school really is, and what it stands for.

Unfortunately, the language and the concept of "school culture" are still mysterious, remote, or alien to many school administrators. The sociology of the organization isn't anything that some principals and superinten-dents understand, think about, worry about, or attempt to influence. They assume that whatever kind of culture their school has just happened, or resulted from forces beyond their control—and isn't too critical anyway. Of course, they're making a colossal mistake. Sometimes, it's a career-buster.

As it turns out, the culture, more than any other single factor, deter-mines the ultimate success or failure of any school, including yours.

This was a lesson reinforced for me several years ago during a visit to a high school in Albuquerque, New Mexico. The school was in an old, somewhat worse-for-wear building. It served a low-income minority pop-ulation. Its budget was the same as all the other high schools in the city. It followed the same curriculum as the other schools. Its staff didn't differ significantly from other staffs. On the surface, there was nothing particu-lar to distinguish this school from its sister schools throughout the district.

Nevertheless, this school had been singled out and recognized by the federal government as a National School of Excellence. Its track record of student growth and achievement had caught the eye of federal officials, who identified it as an exemplary Blue Ribbon School—a model for other high schools across the nation to follow.

What accounted for the school's success and star status? An unusually powerful and positive organizational culture. The only thing this school had more of than other comparable schools in the city was a shared culture of commitment, pride, hard work, mutual support, trust, and hope that extended beyond the school walls and into the entire community. A strong culture was enough to elevate the school above its counterparts.

Of course, this one school's singular success wasn't a once-in-a-lifetime phenomenon. Similar examples of culture-driven high performance occur in most cities. You probably have one or more in your own district. It could be your school. The point is, culture matters in schools and all organizations.

Every group or human institution (e.g., family, clan, neighborhood, Scout troop, street gang, bridge club, Red Hat Society, corporation, or labor union) has its own unique internal culture. This culture is often described as the "personality," "character," or "ethos" of the organization. Schools are no exception. If the school has a soul—and I believe it does—that soul resides in its culture.

What's confusing to school administrators is that some well-intentioned authors unduly complicate the notion of organizational culture by drawing on highly technical definitions that only a scientist or anthropologist can appreciate and by making fine distinctions between similar terms (e.g., "culture" and "climate"). It doesn't have to be that complex.

Obviously, most school leaders aren't scientists; so for the practical purposes of this book, a much looser and simpler definition is both useful and helpful.

In this context, the term "culture" is used synonymously with descriptors such as the "climate," "atmosphere," or "environment" within the school. Other observers have defined the school's culture as the "architecture of the invisible," the "social memory," or the "hidden curriculum." Still others merely refer to it as the "Fourth 'R' (Relationships)." Without splitting hairs over definitions, you get the idea.

Whatever you call it, the culture is an unwritten code of conduct. My dictionary defines it as "socially transmitted behavior patterns" made up of

Adopted folkways	Sacred cows
Assumptions	Shared lore
Ethical definitions	Standards
Legends	Traditions
Mores	Unstated purposes
Myths	Work ethics
Priorities	

These elements give every school a special style, temperament, feeling, and tone all its own that constitute its one-of-a-kind culture

This culture (good or bad) is maintained, sustained, transmitted, and perpetuated through its handed-down customs, history, stories, heroes, rituals, ceremonies, celebrations, special events, mascots, logos, slogans, mottoes, symbols, and symbolic acts. Sometimes, even the name of the school announces the culture found inside (e.g., St. John's Military Academy, Marcy Open School, Downtown Prep School).

Most cultures also boast their own scribes, storytellers, protectors, keepers of the flame, and at least one self-appointed "conscience" of the organization. You can probably pick out who plays these parts in your school.

But you can't learn about your school's culture or any other school's culture from publications or official pronouncements. Cultures usually aren't written down.

Nevertheless, everyone in the organization knows what the culture is and actually helps create, preserve, and fine-tune it. The culture's framework of prescribed patterns of behavior and expectations are continuously invented, reinvented, discovered, developed, adopted, or adapted by all the participants over time.

It's no surprise, then, that a school's culture is more than the sum of its parts and takes on a life of its own. It shapes individual and group conduct and defines what's important, what's possible, what's expected, what's accepted, what's preferred, what's praised, what's tolerated, what's encouraged or discouraged, what's rewarded, what's punished, what's taboo, who's up, who's down, and who's allowed to play (and win) within the organization. It is the culture that gives life within the school its meaning, passion, and purpose.

More than anything else, the culture's informal guides to behavior dictate the way people (students and adults) act and interact (sometimes even how they dress), what they talk about (or don't talk about) in the student commons or the faculty lounge, what approaches to instruction are valued, how teachers perceive students and vice versa, how people treat each other, what motivates both teachers and learners, and how people go about their work every day. In many ways, every school is a captive of its own culture.

Obviously, culture concerns are heady stuff, much too important for any self-respecting school leader to deny, ignore, or just let happen. If you're a principal or superintendent, it pays to pay attention to the culture of the organization. Period!

If you want to know who has the real power in your school, how things really get done, and what it takes to go along and get along within the organization, you won't find the answers in the official rules, job descriptions, discipline code, union contract, or staff handbook. The only way to learn these things is to figure out the culture and how it works. One of the best-kept success secrets for school leaders is to get to know how the culture within your organization actually operates and to use the culture to your advantage.

There is no question that adult and student behaviors alike are heavily influenced by the culture in which they teach and learn. Cultures aren't carved in stone. Cultures are interactive. They are shaped by the people who make up the culture, and, in turn, the participants are shaped by the very culture they helped produce.

Cultures are also elastic and organic. They can be stretched. They can grow and change. As a school leader, you can be bound by the existing culture. Or you can do the stretching and nurturing of growth. But you can't be successful completely independent of the organization's unwritten rules and cultural imperatives.

Sadly, some school officials spend their entire careers completely oblivious and unaware of the culture and how things really work in their own department, school, or district. We've all known administrators who come to the job every day without a clue about what's going on around them. It's almost as if they live and work in some parallel universe rather than in the real world of the school.

I'm reminded of a former superintendent of mine who felt that the primary function of his job was to relate to his immediate employer—the school board. Consequently, he intentionally devoted 60 percent or more of his time to serving and servicing board members. Everyone else (kids, teachers, parents, and community members) had to take a backseat and wait their turn.

His approach to the superintendency may have been good politics, but it was bad for the overall climate within the organization. It didn't help that his obsession with the school board made him appear aloof and disdainful of other stakeholders. Because he distanced himself from everyday relationships and dynamics at the school level, things pretty much had to bump along without his engagement.

Quicker than you would think possible, morale took a nosedive. People felt a bit abandoned. Many grew uneasy and resentful. Throughout the district, there was a lot of frustration, some tension, and even a little fear. And any sense of a "culture of collaboration" rapidly evaporated.

Some called this period the "dark ages" of the district. It may have been less than coincidence that during this time, voters rejected a levy referendum for the first time in the history of the school system.

Of course, the board-consumed superintendent eventually moved on, and a new era was ushered in. Through fate or design, he was followed by a school leader who championed grassroots involvement, open communication, and decentralized decision making. Unlike his predecessor, the replacement felt that part of his job was to lead, educate, and even discipline the school board when necessary, not merely to serve it.

It should come as no surprise that things quickly returned to "normal," and a more cohesive culture reemerged under this new leadership. And subsequent bond issues passed easily. If you think there's a take-home lesson for all of us here, you're right!

It was a different (but just as instructive) story for another urban superintendent I knew, who had the misfortune to follow a predecessor known for visibility, accessibility, and inclusiveness. By contrast, shortly after taking over, the newcomer told one of her principals that she didn't have time to meet and mingle with the teachers standing close by during a visit to his school. Naturally, the story of the brush-off spread almost instantaneously throughout the district.

Soon after, at a meeting of district principals, the new superintendent responded to an administrator's request for clarification by turning away from the questioner and saying to other principals nearby, "Did you understand what I said? Then you explain it to him. I don't have time to repeat it." Wouldn't you know—this story also made the rounds of all the schools in record time.

Surprisingly (?), despite improved test scores, this tact-deprived superintendent lasted only 18 months. Could it have had anything to do with being totally out of touch with the prevailing culture of the district?

Even more blatant, perhaps, may have been the misstep of another newly hired superintendent in my old hometown, who announced, even before his first official day on the job, that "There will be no classroom parties next year." It might be possible to get off to a worse start, but I don't know how. There's nothing quite like debunking an organization's culture before you even show up. Needless to say, this is not a recommended career move for any school official.

If you think these cases seem a little extreme or isolated, a more common example—one all of us have witnessed in some form—is the principal who is always bragging about the "family" atmosphere in his school, while in reality everyone knows that the staff is riddled with dissent, and the principal himself is viewed as a bully.

If you haven't noticed this kind of disconnect between what is said and what is real, you're not paying attention. Of course, a culture based on denial never fools anyone. It is frequently a surefire recipe for early departure.

Administrators like those above, who are not in tune with the culture of the school, quickly become irrelevant. They don't matter. At best, they are ignored or patronized. They aren't really leading anyone or anything anywhere, and don't even know it. (Usually, no one has the heart to tell them that they are no longer running the school.) Instead, staff members merely tolerate their presence and pretty much do things their own way. You don't want this to happen on your watch. As an old mentor once told me, "If the train leaves without you, you can't rightly call yourself the engineer."

In the final analysis, how people in any organization feel about the organization, themselves, their work, their leaders, and their future is largely the result of the culture. As leader, unless you have a handle on the culturally embedded beliefs, behaviors, and biases within the school, you are deprived of a powerful and essential leadership tool.

At the risk of repetition, it is the school's culture that determines how honest people are, how happy they are, how hard they will work, how loyal they will be, and how much they will put up with. Likewise, it is the culture that attracts people to the organization—or drives them away. In short, a school can be only as good as its culture allows it to be.

This culture thing is a huge deal. As leader, you deny or downplay it at your peril. Your only real choices are to embrace the culture, enter into it, reinforce it, adjust it or adjust to it, challenge it, or work to mold, shape, redirect, or reinvent it—or sit on the sidelines—but you can't simply ignore it and remain in charge.

Naturally, all administrators want the most affirming, actualizing, positive, productive, rewarding, and inspiring culture possible, not just for students but for teachers, parents, and the overall community as well. The best school cultures work for everyone. Such an inclusive, fully functioning culture can make your school not just another choice for students and parents but the best choice. Do you want to settle for anything less?

In practice, every principal and superintendent you've ever known or heard about claims to have created a school culture based on service, integrity, equality, compassion, teamwork, and academic excellence (and perhaps "truth, justice, and the American way" as well).

You and I and everyone else in the world know that not all school cultures are alike. They are not always what they seem or claim to be.

There are many ways to be a school. That's why you will find as many kinds of teaching and learning environments as there are separate institutions (see Chapter 2).

Every school looks a little different. And every school acts and reacts differently. The proof of the culture is in the behavior—not in the slogans.

2

The Many Phases and Faces of School Personalities

I call it "Kentucky Fried Schooling." Every school is like a franchise with its own separate set of responsibilities.

—Andy Hargreaves, Boston College

I t's obvious—but it has to be stated anyway—that every single school (past, present, and future) embodies a distinct culture. There are no twins, duplicates, or carbon copies. Like snowflakes, fingerprints, and leaf patterns, no two school environments are exactly alike. The variety is infinite.

If you survived that revelation, you should be ready to accept that some school cultures are healthy (see Chapter 3) and that some are toxic (see Chapter 4).

Some school cultures actually promote the ease and convenience of the adults in the organization over the needs of the children. Other cultures nurture children but impose unreasonable stress and demands on staff members. Still others provide safe havens for students and staff but virtually shut out others (parents and the public).

Worse yet, some cultures actually end up turning kids off, burning out staff members, shutting out parents, and alienating the community all at once. Fortunately, there are other school environments that heal, unite, and galvanize all stakeholders into cohesive action on behalf of kids.

The very best schools in the business, however, boast a culture that aligns the values of the participants with the mission of the organization, while supporting and benefiting everyone involved.

So if there are doubters out there who still think that a school is a school is a school, they've forgotten what school is really like. Look back at the times you changed schools or moved up to the next level of schooling. It felt different each time, didn't it? The climate of a classroom or school is not transferable.

The simple truth is that, like human beings, every school has its own personality. Some even have split personalities. Each school has a distinguishing brand that is stamped on everyone it touches.

What makes education interesting (and sometimes embarrassing) is that school environments can differ in myriad ways. To illustrate the scope of variation, here are a few common examples:

Variations in School Culture

Some School Cultures . . .	Other School Cultures . . .
Emphasize academics	Emphasize the "whole child"
Are data-driven	Are dream-driven
Stress teamwork	Stress individual achievement
Are stratified	Are boundaryless
Welcome change	Resist change
Let outsiders in	Keep outsiders at arm's reach
Practice transparent decision making	Practice closed-door decision making
Centralize authority	Decentralize power and responsibility
Feature a hierarchy	Feature a flat organization
Honor the past	Worship the future
Follow rules	Break rules
Look outside for solutions	Look inward for answers
Admit mistakes	Deny any fault
Punish failure	Reward effort
Decide what kids need	Ask kids what they need

And here's my personal favorite, coined by William Bridges in *The Character of Organizations* (2000).

Some School Cultures . . .	Other School Cultures . . .
Are "stuck in the mud"	Are "lost in the clouds"

The list could go on and on, but you get the point. School cultures vary endlessly in substance and style.

The tricky part is that differences don't necessarily denote that one culture is superior to another. Sometimes, cultures are just different. They can be separate but equally effective. When it comes to school environments, there is no one size that fits all. No single personality type works best for all schools or is "right" for all circumstances. You know this from your own observation and experience, and so do I.

I once worked in a highly regarded and successful suburban school district known for its open, informal, and innovative culture—a culture that embraced individual creativity and encouraged staff members to bring back at least "one crazy idea" from every conference or workshop they attended.

At the same time, a neighboring district, also widely acclaimed for its excellence, featured an entirely different teaching and learning environment. It was more "buttoned up" and traditional. Its culture valued formalized procedures, detailed policies, and specific rules. Personnel, at all levels, were expected to do things "by the book," and the school had a huge policy manual to prove it.

Although they represented radically different cultures (they occasionally even lost talent to each other as individuals sought their own comfort levels), both districts flourished, and for good reason.

The district where I worked served an inner-ring suburb and had to scramble to accommodate changing demographics and increasing diversity, while maintaining its track record of high achievement and avoiding the abyss of declining performance found in some urban, inner-city school settings.

The neighboring district represented a "farther out" suburb with a less diverse and more stable, settled, and conservative clientele. As it turned out, both districts probably had the cultures that they deserved and that best fit their unique niches.

Obviously, effective school leaders strive to determine what type of culture best suits their situation, and then work to create that type of environment; but it's more complicated than that.

We've all heard of people with multiple personalities. Surprise! Organizations can be the same way. Most organizational cultures are mosaics or collages—composites of component cultures. For example, a school district constitutes an overall (super) culture; but it is made up of a variety of subcultures, including classrooms, departments, and individual schools—each with its own identity. And they aren't necessarily all "in sync" (e.g., elementary and secondary schools often reflect different values).

You can witness this coexistence of subcultures simply by following secondary school students moving from class to class during the school day. It's not uncommon for the same student to exhibit different personas in different classes. I've seen students who were reserved in one class and outgoing in the next, serious one hour and the class clown in another, or flirty one period and shy the next. It's not that the student's basic personality changes hourly; it's that each class has a unique chemistry and a different character, which evokes different responses and behaviors.

It's the school leader's responsibility to get the various subcultures all on the same page in support of the greater vision and overall culture. Unfortunately, this can be like trying to herd cats. Nevertheless, it has to be done or the organization is in chaos. More about this later (see Chapters 7 and 8).

Here's another wrinkle. Whatever culture or cultures exist in your organization, they are not going to last. Organizational climates change in subtle—and not-so-subtle—ways over time. If you've been in this business very long, you've observed schools assuming different personalities during different periods of development.

Since cultures are organic, there is a certain natural progression that most organizations experience, whether they are nations, businesses, nonprofit agencies, or schools. Although it's not cast in concrete, or even in plaster of Paris, most cultures evolve through the following phases. The progression may be telescoped, but seldom are steps omitted entirely.

The Life Cycle of a School Culture

1. *Embryonic Stage*	Pursuing an identity. Casting around for the right niche. Trying on different personalities to see what fits.
2. *Cohesion*	Coming together. Consensus on shared values.
3. *Institutionalization*	Embedding beliefs and customs into policy and written or formal procedures.
4. *Loosening of Ties*	Habit replaces passion. Questioning. Second-guessing. Weakening of commitment.
5. *New Beginnings*	Waffling. False starts. Being pulled in different directions. Some resistance to change. Drive the wagons in a circle.
6. *Midcourse Correction*	Tweaking. Redefinition. Or Redirection.
7. *Repeat the Cycle*	

To better understand why organizational cultures evolve and change, it helps to look at the multitude of forces that impinge on and shape the environment. The culture of a school, as with other organizations, doesn't just happen. Where does it come from?

The personality of your school—or any other school—is the result of the collision and interaction of many factors. Here's a partial list:

- Original mandate (stated purpose of the organization)
- History (benchmarks, milestones, and turning points)
- Economics and politics (local, state, and national)
- Legal requirements, regulations, and restrictions: the three R's (e.g., No Child Left Behind legislation)
- Court decisions (e.g., *Brown v. Board of Education of Topeka*)
- External events (e.g., Sputnik, 9/11)
- Changing demographics
- Social trends, fashions, and fads
- New research findings (learning theory, child development)
- Attacks, threats, and challenges
- The competition (Sometimes, what others do prescribes what your organization becomes.)
- Changes in leadership

The list could be much longer, but this should be sufficient to drive home the point. Cultures change. They have to. They can't not change, because they are susceptible to all the dynamic influences, forces, and factors above—and more.

Some of these determiners are fixed and static. Others are fluid. But even the fixed influences can be reinterpreted and manipulated. These, then, are the primary elements you have to work with to improve your school climate.

Some of these factors you can control. Many you cannot. Of course, the element you can control the most is the leadership—your leadership. Fortunately, these are no small potatoes.

Look at the schools you know best. They are all different. Some may be closed, rigid, inflexible, and oppressive. Others may be open, empowering, flexible, and upbeat. What makes the difference? Often, it is the leader.

From the vantage point of an extended career, I have observed firsthand the impact of leadership on the culture of a single school district. Over time, the district's culture has been reinvented in many forms, shadings, and nuances under the leadership of six separate superintendents, with tenures ranging from 2 to 24 years. On the following page, see how it worked:

A History of Superintendents and Their Cultures

Leadership Style	Organizational Culture
1. Paternalistic. Low-key. "Old school."	Formal. Traditional. Valued integrity and an old-fashioned work ethic.
2. Formal. Aloof. Controlling. No-nonsense. Meticulous. Maintained distance and an "administrative mystique."	By-the-books. Cautious. Conservative. Concerned with detail. Observable tension and paranoia.
3. Charismatic. Open. Informal. Visionary. Innovative.	Excitement. Passion. Creativity. Valued risk taking and "pushing the envelope."
4. Unpretentious. Cheerleader. Transparent—"What you see is what you get." Easy-going.	Nonthreatening. Relaxed. Comfortable. Self-proclaimed "family atmosphere."
5. Dedicated. Tireless. Caring. Authentic. Unassuming. Hands-on. Accessible.	Inspired. Motivated. Positive. Mutually supportive.
6. Machiavellian. Vindictive. Distrustful. Distanced.	Don't take chances. Hunker down. Keep a low profile. CYA ("Cover Your Anchovies").

Of course, many factors contributed to the cultural shifts in the example above. But nobody with an IQ equal to their age would dispute that these changes had to be due in large part to the leadership at the top.

Just as in the example, all school cultures are constantly growing, morphing, reforming, adjusting, and adapting. Organizations can learn. When they do, the internal environment is altered—sometimes without the people in the culture even realizing it.

The best news for school leaders: cultures are malleable. They are continuously being shaped and sculpted by a mixture of influences, not the least of which is the impact of administrative example and direction. In short, school personalities show many faces and go through many phases. They can change. School leaders can change them. It's what leaders do. It's something you can do, too (see Chapter 7).

Of course, principals and superintendents can't create a desired organizational culture simply by issuing an executive fiat or administrative edict. Or force unwanted values on people. Or transform ingrained beliefs and behaviors overnight. But they can effect change through teaching, modeling, coaxing, convincing, cajoling, and a host of other overt and covert strategies. It's called leadership. It begins with a vision of what works.

Unfortunately, some school officials wouldn't know an effective school environment if they saw one. Since you have read this far, you obviously don't want to be in that number. So what does a healthy school environment look like?

3

Profile of a Healthy School Culture That Works for Everyone

We want a culture that appreciates yesterday, celebrates today and designs a better tomorrow.

—Jim Benson, past president of Dunwoody College of Technology and Bemidji (MN) State University

───────────── ✧ ─────────────

Is your school's culture constructive, obstructive, or destructive? I promised I would explain the difference, and I will.

But it's not easy to be precise or definitive in spelling out what a healthy school culture looks like. After all, a culture is the elusive, intangible inner reality of the organization; and there are lots of variations, many of which can be positive.

You can find healthy cultures in large schools and in small schools, in schools with new buildings and schools with old buildings, and even in schools with no permanent buildings at all. And you can find good cultures in rich schools and in poor schools and in everything in between. It's not a matter of mortar, masonry, or money. The culture is about the people. More specifically, the culture is about the relationships within the organization.

You can't touch a school's culture—but you can feel it. You've probably had the experience of entering a school for the first time and almost immediately sensing that something's working here.

Since ethos is largely subjective, it sometimes helps to use metaphors to demonstrate more clearly what distinguishes a constructive culture from the rest of the pack. Following are four of my favorite analogies.

In his acceptance speech upon receiving the Nobel Peace Prize at the University of Oslo in 1964, Dr. Martin Luther King, Jr. told the tale of the "World House." In King's story, a widely separated, disparate, diverse, and dysfunctional family inherited a large mansion together—with the proviso that they all had to live in it harmoniously or forfeit the inheritance.

In his address, which later became a chapter in his book *Where Do We Go From Here: Chaos or Community?* (1967), King went on to make the point that the house in the story is a metaphor for our real world today. As a global family, we have inherited the world house, and now all races, creeds, religions, ethnic groups, and social classes have to live in it together and get along or lose it and face disaster.

Later in the speech, King called for all peoples to transcend tribes, races, classes, and religions; eradicate racism; become a people-oriented society; resist social injustice; and learn to resolve conflicts peacefully. So far, the world isn't doing too well in responding to King's admonition. Good schools do much better.

If King's vision is ever to become reality, it will have to start with schoolchildren. That's why the best school cultures everywhere resemble the "World House."

Increasingly, your school is a microcosm of the greater world. What's needed is a school environment that accepts, nurtures, celebrates, and works for everyone.

A constructive school culture is an inclusive culture.

A similar case was made in a 2005 nationwide ad campaign conducted by a major Protestant denomination. The ad showed two burly bouncers (like those found at popular nightclubs across the country) stationed at the entrance of a church to screen those seeking admittance.

During the course of the commercial, the bouncers excluded (rejected) several minority, handicapped, and gay individuals, while admitting White congregants without hesitation. The concluding message was that some churches may bar certain people, but the church sponsoring the ad is open and affirming and never turns anyone away. Separation of church and state notwithstanding, good schools are a lot like the denomination that sponsored this ad.

Of course, unlike churches, public schools have to admit everyone. The question then becomes, Does the school culture really accept and support all pupils with equal vigor, high expectations, attention, compassion, and enthusiasm?

Schools with the most positive and productive environments pull out all the stops for all kids—not just for the White kids, the bright kids, the clean kids, the well-behaved kids, or the kids who look and talk just like their teachers.

A constructive school culture is an equal-opportunity culture.

This point is again illustrated, and carried one step further, in the story of the "wooden bowl," which has embellished countless sermons in churches across the country. According to this story, an old grandfather, who was palsied and suffered from Alzheimer's disease, lost his wife and had to go live with his son's family. Unfortunately, the family was not happy about the intrusion.

Mealtime became a problem. The old man drooled a lot, and his shaking often caused him to spill food. The children complained about having to eat with him. They didn't like to watch him struggle through a meal. The parents agreed that it wasn't a pretty sight.

One day, the old man accidentally knocked his bowl off the table, spilled his soup, and broke the dish. This was the last straw. The family decided that Grandfather should start eating alone, out of an unbreakable wooden bowl, at a separate table, out of sight. It worked for a while. And the family felt that mealtimes were much more pleasant with Grandfather absent.

Then, one evening, the father came home to find his little boy whittling on some pieces of wood. "What are you doing?" he asked. The boy replied, "I'm making wooden bowls for you and Mom to use when you get old."

The boy's statement stunned the father and caused him and his wife to rethink their behavior and the message they were sending to their children. They decided to invite Grandfather back to the table to be part of the family at mealtime again.

Wow! This story has lessons on many levels for families—and for schools. Of course, public schools have to let everyone in the door; but do they truly let everyone into their culture? Often, there are certain students and families whom some teachers and administrators would prefer not to work with—people they would like to relegate to a separate table somewhere out of sight—but that's not an option.

In good schools, everyone is invited to the table—everyone is part of the family.

In a constructive school culture, there are no second-class citizens.

A different insight on cultures was underscored for me by a recent experience in a hospital rehabilitation center. For a short period, my wife had to go to a

(Continued)

(Continued)

nearby hospital several times a week for physical and occupational therapy. On these occasions, I spent the time sitting in the lobby area observing people come and go.

The lobby entrance area was staffed by three greeters and a couple of receptionists at an information desk. Everyone who came to the rehab center was met at the curb or at the door by one of the greeters, who offered them a wheelchair and volunteered to wheel them anywhere in the hospital they wanted to go.

Both the greeters and the receptionists were quick to put people at ease, answer questions, and help in any way possible. On one occasion, I saw an elderly woman slip and fall outside near the door. Within nanoseconds, three staff members surrounded and assisted her.

Over time, I watched countless people come through the doors. Many were hurting, scared, and nervous. Almost immediately, they were observably calmed and, often, surprised by the attention they received. Universally, they expressed appreciation and gratitude for the unexpected assistance.

I told one of the greeters, "You have the best job in the world. You spend all day helping people and getting appreciative feedback for your efforts." He agreed.

My vigil extended over several weeks at different times of day. The atmosphere of commitment and caring never wavered.

Every school should be more like a rehab unit where everyone who enters, regardless of age or station in life, feels welcomed and has their needs anticipated and addressed by dedicated professionals—without waiting, without asking, and without being judged.

Actually, many schools already are like that. God bless 'em.

A constructive school culture welcomes everyone, exceeds expectations, and values exceptional service.

These four vignettes—about a house, a church, a family, and a hospital—symbolize the essence of what constitutes a constructive school culture; but there's more to it. Much more.

It bears repeating, however, that it is risky to be overly specific in describing a healthy school personality. As soon as you start naming exact features that are essential for an effective school environment, along comes a successful school that doesn't have them.

For example, the Metropolitan Regional Career and Technical Center ("the Met"), a high school in Providence, Rhode Island, must have something going for its culture. The school serves a population made up of about 50 percent minorities and 60–80 percent low-income pupils. Despite this, in 2004, the school had only a 2–3 percent dropout rate, and 100 percent of its graduates were accepted into college. And it accomplished all this with no formal curriculum, no grades, no tests, no gym teacher, no music teacher, and no librarian. Obviously, you can't define a winning school culture simply by its organization, structure, or traditional trappings.

The definition of a healthy school culture has to be as fluid, flexible, amorphous, and adaptable as . . . well, as a healthy school culture.

Even though there is no one foolproof formula, there are certain absolutes or truths that apply to all the most effective and productive school environments. Feel free to use the list below to keep score on your own school.

The Truth—and Nothing But . . .

A healthy school culture works for everyone. It is a complete package that feeds the needs of all constituencies and stakeholders (e.g., students, staff, parents, and community members). As a former administrator and old friend of mine once described it, "The school reaches out and offers something nutritious for everyone from preschool to graduation and beyond."

A healthy school culture balances the interests of the one, the few, and the many. For example, the culture decentralizes decision making, while maintaining a unified, central focus. Likewise, it rewards individual achievement and encourages teamwork at the same time.

A healthy school culture is principle-driven. It values principles over personalities or procedures. It is only upon principles that any organizational culture can be built to last.

There will always be intermittent bad times, budget crises, lackluster leaders, personnel turnover, paranoid parents, cost-conscious communities, weak school boards, and punitive legislatures. Adherence to core principles at all costs enables a culture to persist through good times, bad times, and all the times in between.

A healthy school culture stresses relationships and connections. It strengthens everyone's sense of affiliation with the school and enhances rich, supporting, and energetic relationships among all those involved.

A healthy school culture is a learning culture. Without opportunities for relentless renewal, a culture chooses death. Learning works only if the growth opportunities are extended to everyone in the school—not just teachers and administrators, but aides, clerks, cooks, custodians, and even bus drivers as well.

(Continued)

(Continued)

A healthy school culture makes respect and individual dignity a priority. One of my favorite anecdotes about respect was reported in the Retired Educators Association of Minnesota (REAM) newsletter by retired teachers Bob and LuBell Kendall, who spent time teaching in China. At first, the Kendalls wondered why their Chinese students didn't get up and leave when the classes were over. They were accustomed to American pupils, who signal the approaching end of the period by restless shifting and shuffling, closing their books, and gathering up their materials.

By contrast, the Chinese students didn't rattle papers, stand up, or make a move when it was time to leave. Eventually, the Kendalls learned that Chinese students don't budge until the teacher announces, "The class is over." Anything less would be considered disrespectful. As the Kendalls explained, "We never felt so respected."

A healthy school culture makes the mission *the definition of success.* A well-crafted *mission,* shared vision, and clear expectations help everyone "keep the main thing the main thing." When individual and organizational success are synonymous, look out, world. Big things are about to happen!

A healthy school culture values freedom. Students and adults alike are free to use their talents and to exercise some control over their jobs. In return, people are expected to take responsibility for their actions and to exercise self-discipline.

A healthy school culture is a transparent culture. The culture is based on open communication and a free flow of information in all directions. (Some writers call it a "honeycomb" of communication.) Bare-knuckle exchanges of opinion and ideas are allowed; and few, if any, subjects are taboo or off the table.

Meetings are open. So is the budget. Most important, everyone knows what's happened, what's going on, and what's coming up.

A healthy school culture holds expectations of excellence, high performance, and exceptional service. Mediocrity is unacceptable. Giving up on success or on each other is not part of the bargain.

If you've read Mark Sanborn's inspirational book *The Fred Factor* (2005), you know that Fred was an extraordinary postman who did much more than deliver the mail. He cared for the people on his route. He looked after their homes while they were away, delivered important packages after hours, and exceeded expectations in unexpected ways.

Every constructive culture has to have a large measure of the Fred Factor. There's a little bit of Fred in every effective school leader.

A healthy school culture is fear-free or, at least, fear-reduced. Students and staff feel safe enough to try and to fail and to try again—and to succeed.

A healthy school culture values sharing. Collegiality, collaboration, and sharing experiences are expectations, not exceptions.

A healthy school culture tends to be "Goldilocksian." Not too big, not too small. Not too hot, not too cold. Not too hard, not too soft—but just right!

The most productive school environments are radical about kids and achievement but value moderation and persistence in most matters. Success accrues more often to the persistent plodder than to the radical flash in the pan.

A healthy school culture is a fair culture. Equity and justice are core beliefs. The organization is aware of and guards against its own institutional biases and prejudices. Best of all, people believe in and play by the same rules.

A healthy school culture is a place of joy. Humor is a welcome visitor. People have fun. They work hard, have problems, make mistakes, mess up, and miss out—but they are having the time of their lives at the same time.

Having fun is good for people. It strengthens the immune system, stimulates endorphin production, and increases energy. Better yet, having fun is also good for the entire organization.

Fun promotes creativity, builds teams, and relieves tension. Fun and humor together are proven boredom-busters. Having fun gives everyone in the organization another reason to like each other.

A healthy school culture is driven by passion. People care—a lot!

All the stakeholders in a passionate culture are highly motivated because what they do is more than a job—it's a calling! They work hard and give themselves fully, because they feel part of something greater than themselves.

———— ✁ ————

Organizations cannot survive with too many people who don't care or care about the wrong things.

—Leonard O. Pellicer, Dean
School of Education and
Organizational Leadership,
University of La Verne

A healthy school culture creates an aura of excitement ("aliveness"). People in a peak-performing culture exude exuberance (a high state of energy and optimism) and a sense of urgency (what Louis V. Gerstner, former CEO at 3M, calls "constructive impatience").

Exuberance is contagious enthusiasm that motivates people at all levels to take risks and overcome setbacks. It is a hook into the future. That's why the best cultures you know about are "alive" with wonder and discovery. It's what separates winners from wannabes.

A healthy school culture radiates confidence. It assumes success.

(Continued)

(Continued)

Derek Leebaert, author of *To Dare and to Conquer* (2006), explains that the only way the vastly outnumbered Spanish Conquistadors were able to conquer the entire Aztec empire was because the Spanish warriors had ". . . complete self-assurance and utter faith in one's fellows—that multiplied the clout of constant improvisation." Good school cultures share that same sense of self-assurance. It emboldens them. It's how they persevere. A little bravado goes a long way.

A healthy school culture is consistent. An empowering culture brings out the best in everyone—not just when someone important shows up, not just when the media is around, and not just on good days—but every day!

A healthy school culture maintains perspective. A positive culture survives because it holds to the long view. The culture refuses to panic or resort to knee-jerk reactions or stopgap measures under pressure.

Abe Lincoln told the story of an Eastern monarch who challenged his country's wisest counselors to craft a sentence that would be true and appropriate at all times and in all situations. The learned advisers finally came up with the sentence, "This, too, shall pass away."

These are words to live by for all those working and learning in a fully functioning school culture. Such cultures last and outlast other cultures because they are able to keep things in perspective.

That's it: a starter list of absolutes applicable to all healthy school cultures.

These 20 "truths" may not be immutable laws for culture building, but they come as close as you are going to get in this lifetime. If you ever find a school environment somewhere that works for everyone and doesn't evidence these verities, you've discovered a new species. Report it immediately to Ripley's Believe It or Not.

Of course, if this list is too unwieldy, there are shorter versions. For example, in his blockbuster bestseller, *The Purpose-Driven Life*, Rick Warren (2007) writes about the nine characteristics of Biblical fellowship, including

1. Authenticity (sharing true feelings)

2. Mutuality (encouraging each other)

3. Sympathy (supporting each other)

4. Mercy (forgiving each other)

5. Honesty (speaking the truth)

6. Humility (admitting mistakes)

7. Courtesy (respecting differences)

8. Confidentiality (avoiding gossip)

9. Frequency (making the group a priority)

Look again. This is just a telescoped, reordered rendition of the longer list. It's all the stuff good cultures everywhere are made of. You can't have a completely healthy school environment unless everyone involved experiences these nine characteristics. They're givens.

Can it be made any simpler? Maybe. Even though it is difficult to synthesize these varied insights into a single statement of universal truth about what makes a healthy culture, it basically boils down to this:

> Everyone in a winning culture feels like a volunteer. They are where they want to be, doing what they want to do, and doing their best, because they believe what they do is incredibly worthwhile.

When all these pieces are fitted together, a profile of a healthy culture that works for everyone begins to emerge. So if you're interested in an optimum ethos that will set your organization apart and make your school better than most, here's what it should look like:

> Think of the best possible learning environment for kids that you can imagine. A school where every child is known and cared about; where excellence is prized, hard work is recognized, and fun is a priority; where students pull for each other and take care of each other; where something interesting and exciting is happening all the time and everyone wants to show up every day.
>
> Where everyone's contribution is appreciated and no one falls through the cracks; where everyone feels they belong; where people do their best because everyone else is; where being different is OK and being yourself is mandatory; where people can try, fail, try harder, fail better, and eventually succeed; where information is freely shared and problems are squarely faced.
>
> Where success is assumed because it always happens sooner or later; where people are positive, hopeful, and optimistic; where kids compete and cooperate with equal intensity; where encouragement and support are givens; and where expectations are realistic, rules are reasonable, and common sense is contagious.
>
> Now replicate that kind of environment or grown-ups. Voila! You have a winning culture. . . .

> —Robert D. Ramsey, author of *School Leadership From A to Z* (2003)

Now that you have a solid description of what a superior school environment looks like, your next question should be, "How do I get me one?" How does a school leader create a culture that benefits everyone and prompts peak performances at all levels?

Subsequent chapters will spell out a full spectrum of specific strategies, initiatives, and action plans for shaping a culture that works equally well for all students, staff members, parents, and common, garden-variety citizens at the same time.

For now, check out the seven generic starter suggestions below. They're fail-safe. They work every time, and you can implement them starting tomorrow morning.

1. DECLARE WAR ON RUDENESS

Insist on civility and reasonable etiquette at all levels. Following a code of etiquette says a lot about the character and class of an organization (and its leader), is an expression of respect, and creates an atmosphere that signals that everyone is valued.

It can start by reintroducing the language of civility ("Please," "Thank you," "You're welcome," "Excuse me" . . .) into the culture.

It's also the leader's responsibility to model appropriate behavior (e.g., listening politely, refraining from interrupting others, and disagreeing respectfully) and to extend the code of etiquette to all forms of communication and interaction, inside and outside of the organization, including e-mail, voice mail, and text messages.

There's a reason why many business schools are now offering courses in etiquette and many communities have initiated afterschool programs to teach good manners to kids.

When adults and students treat each other with respect, everything goes smoother and better. Common courtesy is the cornerstone of all great cultures.

2. WALK THE TALK

The best way to contribute to a culture of integrity in the workplace is to act with integrity. . . .

—Roland S. Barth
educational author and consultant

"Practice what you preach." Remember your old Sunday school teacher saying something about that? It's still good advice; and it doesn't cost a thing.

Everyone agrees that it's important to demonstrate authenticity and integrity; but what does that mean? Simply, living your values, keeping promises, and doing what you say you're going to do.

How difficult is that? Apparently, very difficult, considering the many leaders in business and politics who fall short. Schools can do better.

Failing to walk the talk sends a wrong message, makes a mockery of your *mission,* and discredits your back-to-school pep talk. After all, the culture of the school isn't what you say it is. It's how you and others act every day.

3. BORROW FROM THE MEDICAL MODEL (E.G., TRIAGE, DIAGNOSIS, PRESCRIPTION, AND TREATMENT)

There are lots of things wrong with America's health care system. But it does one thing right—slashing the time between identifying what needs fixing and starting remediation.

Schools can do the same—and without the elaborate insurance forms and the gowns that gap in the back.

4. MAKE IT OKAY (SOCIALLY ACCEPTABLE) TO MAKE MISTAKES

I first learned about the power of permitting mistakes or failures when I was in kindergarten. Like most five-year-olds, I desperately wanted to please my teacher. When she announced one day that we were short of crayons and asked each of us to bring a box "for crayons" the next day, I listened. And remembered.

I didn't quite understand how boxes would help, but who was I to question the teacher? For all I knew, maybe she wanted to sort out the nearly new, fat crayons and usable stubs from the useless fragments. Anyway, I was ready to do my share.

That night shortly before bedtime, I told my mother what I needed. She didn't understand the teacher's request either, but went along anyway. On short notice, though, the best she could come up with was a large shoebox.

The next morning, I arrived at school a few minutes late. As I entered the classroom, all the other students stopped short and stared at my shoebox in awe and said almost in unison, "Is that your box of crayons? All we have are these little boxes!"

> *Mistakes are not the spice of life. Mistakes are life. Mistakes are not to be tolerated. They are to be encouraged. And, mostly the bigger the better.*
>
> —Tom Peters, business guru

The light dawned. My heart sank. The teacher wanted boxes *of* crayons. All the other kids had brought brand-new boxes of Crayolas. And I was standing there, in the full glare of attention, holding an *empty box!*

I was devastated. I turned, ran out of the classroom, and placed the cursed cardboard container under the tire of a parked car, so it would be crushed for its role in my humiliation. Then, I climbed to the top of the playground jungle gym, sat there, and cried.

Fortunately, my teacher came to find me, coaxed me down, and retrieved the dreaded shoebox. (God bless her. I wish I could remember her name.) Next, she made a big deal out of telling me—and the entire class—all the great uses she had for such a wondrous box.

I was redeemed. A near catastrophe was averted. I wasn't disgraced after all. My teacher not only helped me save face, she helped me gain face with my peers.

That teacher's response said a lot about her humanity, her skill as a teacher, and, most of all, the culture of her classroom. Who wouldn't want their child in that kind of protective, supportive, and affirming environment—where it's okay to make mistakes?

The principle of forgiving (and even celebrating) mistakes applies to adults as well as to children. The truth is, if you can't afford to be wrong, you can't afford to try anything new. Who wants a culture like that?

5. CELEBRATE TOGETHER—EARLY AND OFTEN

Celebrations boost morale, promote unity, and create recognition—and they're fun. What school couldn't use more of that?

> *There isn't enough celebrating going on at work—anywhere.*
>
> —Jack Welch
> legendary CEO of GE

I once worked in a district office where we took time to celebrate each person's birthday with a short party, a card shower, and cake all around. We celebrated the superintendent's birthday. We celebrated the custodian's birthday and the part-time clerk's birthday. Everyone got recognized.

It happened frequently. It took a little time out of the workday; but it boosted spirits, boosted camaraderie, and perhaps even boosted productivity.

Years later, I revisited the office. Of course, things had changed. Turnover had occurred. Several superintendents had come and gone. They no longer celebrated birthdays. For those people who could remember the celebrations, they were missed. A little bit of the culture had died.

6. SURPRISE PEOPLE

A culture can't rock if it becomes too routine. To stay relevant and interesting, avoid the ho-hums and keep everyone excited and engaged; it pays to do the unusual, unexpected, unorthodox, and extraordinary now and then. Surprises keep people on their toes and stimulate greater effort.

Remember the 2005 blockbuster documentary film, *Mad Hat Ballroom,* about teaching ballroom dancing to fifth graders from tough, minority neighborhoods in New York City? Who would have thought that teaching tango and swing to kids from low-income, often single-parent families would end up teaching them important life lessons about empathy, teamwork, responsibility, confidence, and etiquette as well? Someone tried it, and it changed the culture forever.

Likewise, who would ever think of giving violins to poor students in a small village in the Himalayan foothills of India called Kalimpong? Surprise! It works. The kids make great music, which builds confidence that transfers to other learning.

Sometimes, it takes the unusual to shake things up and make a difference. Everyone likes surprises. A good leader doesn't disappoint them.

7. SIMPLIFY THE ORGANIZATION

A lean organization facilitates a nimble culture. Anything you can do to flatten the bureaucracy, remove layers of approval, and reduce the distance between administration and students contributes to a healthier culture.

Theologians and philosophers often talk about "Occam's Razor" (also spelled "Ockham's Razor"), a principle that favors simplicity—a preference for the simplest alternative. Educators should talk about it, too. Good school leaders use Occam's Razor to shave away extraneous and obstructive structures, strictures, rules, and procedures.

There's a reason that the largest and most effective rehabilitation organization in the world, Alcoholics Anonymous, proclaims that it "ought never be organized"; and their leaders are "trusted servants" who do not govern. Schools could learn a lot from the AA culture.

Naturally, these seven starter suggestions won't get you an award-winning, healthy school culture overnight; but they will move your school in the right direction. The sooner you start, the better, because a positive culture not only unleashes the talent of all those within the organization, but also attracts new talent.

Constructive school cultures are magnets for top-notch people, including bright students, highly motivated and involved parents, and gifted teachers who are so good they can teach anywhere. Attracting winners is one way the best school cultures renew and perpetuate themselves.

For me, the classic example of the drawing power of a strong culture came out of a well-known suburban school system near Minneapolis in 2005. One day, officials discovered an immigrant young man who had been living undetected in the high school for some time.

The young immigrant had previously attended the school and liked it. Later, when he found himself without lodging, the school was the safest, most nonthreatening, supportive, and comfortable place he could think of to live.

As a squatter, the immigrant didn't cause any trouble. During the day, he blended in with the other students and even attended some classes. Since his face was somewhat familiar, no one questioned his presence.

For more than three weeks, he ate food from the cafeteria, used an empty locker as a pantry, read and watched TV in the media center, showered in the men's locker room, and slept in the auditorium.

The story didn't have a happy ending for the young man; but it says something about the school's culture. You know you've arrived when the students not only want to come to school every day but also want to actually move in and live there as well.

Of course, not all schools have cultures that attract people to them. Unfortunately, as you know, there are some school environments today so poisonous, obnoxious, and dysfunctional that they literally drive good people away, including influential community supporters.

Want to know what these toxic school cultures look like? That's why we have a Chapter 4.

4

How Do You Know It's Time to Tune Your Bagpipes?

Signs of a Toxic School Culture

You can walk in the door and quickly feel fatigue. They look tired and act tired . . . There is no sense of urgency or excitement.

—John R. Graham, president
Graham Communications

I have found nothing more toxic to a healthy learning environment than an overdose of constant criticism.

—Roland S. Barth
educational author and consultant

———————— �֍ ————————

It must be difficult for a bagpipe player to know when the instrument needs tuning. After all, only a narrow band separates the bagpipe's most melodic tones from an ear-splitting squawk. There is only a fine line between music and noise, and the bagpipe is so loud that it drowns out other instruments that could provide a basis for comparison. Musicians can become so accustomed to the familiar sound of their own instruments that they always seem right on tune.

It can be the same for school administrators in recognizing when the culture of their school is off key or out of pitch. After all, the elements of a healthy and an unhealthy culture are often identical—except that they are out of balance, excessive, or extreme in a toxic environment.

Without exposure to other environments, school leaders can become so closely associated with and used to their own culture that no matter how far out of tune it becomes, it still seems natural and normal. They can't see the forest for the—well, you know the rest.

Let's face it. There are some really lousy school cultures out there. We've all heard horror stories about school environments so bad that they virtually derail learning, damage kids, demoralize teachers, distance parents, and divide communities. And, strangely, the people inside these cultures sometimes don't realize how awful the culture is. Like residents of Chernobyl, it is possible to live, learn, lead, follow, or wallow in a poisonous educational atmosphere and not even know it.

That's why it is important for every principal and superintendent to know the signs and symptoms of a toxic organizational climate. The vision of a healthy school environment becomes clearer and sharper only when viewed in relief against the image of a sick, dysfunctional, or even dying culture.

The problem is that there are many kinds of nasty. Dysfunctional cultures assume varied forms and can be defined, explained, and described in different ways, such as:

> A pervasive and insidious cultural system of beliefs and customs that shape people's lives at all levels (i.e., language, thoughts, feelings, behavior, dreams, expectations, rules, relationships, understandings, lifestyle, politics. . . .)
>
> —Marie-Nathalie Beaudoin and Maureen Taylor, authors
> of *Creating a Positive School Culture* (2004)

> We have made the workplace a frustrating and joyless place where people do what they're told and have few ways to participate in decisions or fully use their talents.
>
> —Dennis W. Bakke, author of *Joy at Work* (2005)

> From the morass of red tape, regulations, forms, files, work rules and mission statements, a huge monster arose. "The Blob," so named by former Secretary of Education, William Bennett, is the impenetrable mass of bureaucracy that crushes creativity, chokes innovation and gobbles up educational funds.
>
> —Joanne Jacobs, author of *Our School* (2005)

Do any of these school environments sound familiar to you? Obviously, a dysfunctional school culture is a many-splintered thing. A wide variety of negative factors and influences contribute to creating a school culture that is unhealthy, unwholesome, and unproductive for everyone.

The examples and descriptors below make the case best of all. (Note: we're not necessarily talking about schools with rundown facilities, tough kids, large classes, guns, gangs, and bad neighborhoods. We're talking about educational and environmental conditions that can—and do—occur in any school, even yours.)

Signs You're Working in the School From Hell

Apathy/complacency

Bureaucratic red tape (forms for everything)

Burnout/counting days to retirement

Busywork/meaningless assignments (worksheet curriculum)

Consumed with testing

Denial/spin-doctoring

Dirty internal politics

Faulty communication/conversations never held

Frequent tears and fears

Fuzzy ethics

Game playing (one-upmanship)

Impersonality

Information hoarding and rationing

Labeling and stereotyping

Obsession with order and neatness

Paranoia/mistrust

Pervasive pessimism

Predictability/boredom

Proliferating rules

Propensity for the past ("good ol' days")

Punitive mentality/discipline by ridicule

Regimentation/emphasis on routine

Rigid hierarchy/inflexible organizational charts and job descriptions

Secrets/hidden agendas

Teacher isolation

Top-down decision making

Turf battles

Undercurrent of complaint/whining

Unreasonable expectations (e.g., "silent lunches")

Unwelcoming atmosphere

Vague goals and roles

Value conformity over creativity

Worshiping false gods/serving the wrong master

Zero tolerance for new ideas

What's missing? Passion, laughter, frivolity, wonder, mystery, fun!

Naturally, the more of these pollutants present in the school, the greater the contamination of the culture. Singly or in small numbers, they are mostly harmless distractions. Probably every school contains some of these elements. But when they accrue or accumulate to become a critical mass, the culture is no longer a healthy environment for teaching and learning.

Of course, not all these negative factors are equally weighted. Some do more damage to more people more quickly than others. Among the worst cultural contaminants with the most crippling effects on any school environment are the following:

1. DENIAL

It's a mistake not to admit mistakes. And it's a bigger mistake to deny the existence of problems. Mistakes and problems ignored don't get fixed. They get worse and more difficult to correct or resolve.

Of course, it's only natural to want to avoid unpleasantness, bad news, and admission of fault or failure. It's natural to want to wish that bad things would just go away. (". . . it is nature to man to indulge in the illusion of Hope. We are apt to shut our eyes against painful truths." —Patrick Henry, voice of the American Revolution.) It's natural, but it's also wrong, unhealthy, stupid, and self-defeating.

Individuals and organizations who traffic in denial end up traveling alone. They not only forfeit their credibility with others, but also end up mistrusting themselves.

Ad-libbing, spin-doctoring, glossing over, looking the other way, sandbagging, and sweeping bad stuff under the rug aren't remedies. They're delusions.

A culture of denial can't get better. It can only get weaker and worse. Enduring cultures solve real problems in the real world in real time.

> *Whether dwelling on a problem, hiding a problem or dribbling out partial answers for a problem while you wait for a high tide to raise your boat, dithering and delay almost always compound a negative situation. . . . The sine qua non of any successful organization is public acknowledgment of the existence of a problem.*
>
> —Louis V. Gerstner, former CEO IBM Corporation, author of *Who Says Elephants Can't Dance?* (2003)

You just can't beat honesty. It's an essential building block for any effective school culture. Admitting and facing up to problems and mistakes is the first step to making things right. There isn't any other first step!

2. BUREAUCRACY

A bureaucratic structure and creativity are almost mutually exclusive because bureaucracies are notoriously impersonal and unfeeling. Worse yet, it's easy for people to become "comfortable" (settle in), lazy, and lethargic in a bureaucracy, but it's difficult to be excited, energized, and innovative. This alone should be enough to convince you that bureaucracy is nasty stuff that you don't want any part of in your school culture.

Louis V. Gerstner describes a bureaucratic environment as "a stultifying culture with a spider web of checks, approvals and validations." As former CEO for the behemoth IBM corporation, he should know.

Bureaucracies are about multiple layers of gatekeepers, overlapping supervision, endless reporting, conformity, regimen, routine, rules, regulations, obese policy manuals, hierarchy, rank, status, power, control, and lots of charts and graphs. Conversely, effective schools are about compassion, hope, excitement, learning, growth, and fun—not just for kids, but for everyone. That's why schools and bureaucracy don't mix.

In any bureaucratic organization,

- It's difficult to get noticed, be recognized, have a voice. or make a difference. (Things trickle down but seldom bubble up.)
- It's difficult to innovate or change anything. (Bureaucracies move at a glacial pace in a fast-forward world.)
- It's difficult to know whom you can trust, what's true, and what's really going on.
- It's difficult not to feel undervalued and unappreciated.
- It's difficult to have any control over what happens to you.
- It's difficult to find something to feel personally proud about.
- It's difficult not to be afraid.

What kind of environment is that for little kids? Or for grown-ups? For you?

The greatest single piece of advice for any school administrator concerned about developing a positive school culture is: *Simplify*—your organization and your life!

3. DIRTY POLITICS

Wherever there are people, there is politics. You can't remove politics from any human institution, even a school; but you can clean it up.

At its worst, organizational politics involves seeking personal gain or advantage through the use of dirty tricks, personal attacks, confidentiality violations, sabotage, or vicious innuendo, gossip, and rumor.

It's interesting that an unknown wag once pointed out that the term "pol" means "people" in Latin and that the term "tic" means "blood-sucking creature." What does that tell you about politics as it plays out in many organizations—and in some schools?

Unfortunately, there are Machiavellian school leaders who resort to dirty politics to gain, retain, or maintain control and to advance their personal agendas. Here's how the French writer Pierre Beaumarchais explains it in *The Marriage of Figaro*:

> It's easy. Pretend to know what you don't and pretend not to know what you do. Hear what you don't understand and don't hear what you do. Promise what you cannot deliver, what you have no intention of delivering. Make a great secret of hiding what isn't there. Plead you're busy as you spend time sharpening pencils. Speak profoundly to cover up your emptiness, encourage spies, reward traitors, tamper with seals, interrupt letters, hide the ineptitude of your goals by speaking of them glowingly—that's all there is to politics, I swear. (Beaumarchais, 1778)

School leaders usually get the culture they deserve. If you lead by employing dirty politics, you're in the wrong business. Change your ways or change your profession. Schools, kids, and communities need (and deserve) real leaders and statesmen, not political hacks and henchmen. There is no place for dirty politics in any school's culture. Period!

4. FEARS

A culture of fear is a culture of "no" (e.g., negativity, rejection, and taboo). It's true that fear is a motivator. But mostly it motivates people to hunker down, avoid risks, keep a low profile, fit in, avoid rocking the boat, and keep feelings and good ideas to themselves. Isn't that just the opposite of what you want in a fully functioning school culture?

If your organization is afraid of exposure, competition, or being found out, and if your students are afraid of failure, punishment, or humiliation, and if your staff is afraid of rebuke or reprisal, and if you're afraid of letting go, you're not running a school, you're operating a prison.

If the people in the organization are afraid of you, you're doing something wrong. Fear can make your school an obstacle, not an avenue to learning. Good school leaders remove obstacles. That includes fear—especially fear.

5. SERVING THE WRONG MASTER

Some schools end up with a toxic culture because they lose their way, misplace their moral compass, forget their mission, or get their priorities mixed up. It happens in all kinds of organizations, including schools. In fact, it occurs a lot in this country.

Popular author and speaker Edith Weiner tells the story of visiting aliens who report back that Earth is inhabited by four-wheeled vehicles who own two-legged slaves. Daily, the slaves take their masters to a social club where the automobiles hang out together, while the human slaves go inside and work to support their four-wheeled masters.

The point is that it's easy to misinterpret or get mixed up about what's true and who or what is most important. Aliens can do it. So can people. So can schools.

If a superintendent thinks his real job is to service the needs of the school board members, or a principal makes pleasing the superintendent the highest priority, or teachers value test scores over everything else, or a community is willing to sacrifice academic excellence for a state football championship, they're worshiping the wrong gods.

Anytime that kids cease to be the greatest priority, with nothing else a close second, the school's culture becomes a little more toxic.

You can't have a healthy school environment unless it's rigged in favor of kids—not just part of the time, but all the time. Anything less is serving the wrong master. If your culture is going south, look first to what your real priorities are. When you lose sight of the real reason the school exists, it's time to tune the bagpipes.

6. APATHY

The most damning indictment of any school culture is, "No one cares anymore." It doesn't get any worse than that. If you and your staff don't care, this book can't help you; and only God can help the children.

Needless to say, the list above is incomplete. But it should be sufficient to exemplify the crippling conditions that lead to a toxic school culture. The next question should be: "How can it happen?" How and why do school cultures turn toxic?

As with most issues in education, the answer lies in the people. Toxic people make toxic cultures. Through intention, inattention, action, passivity, neglect, or default, the people in the organization promote, foster, or allow an unhealthy environment to develop. Often, the leader is a prime suspect.

> *The opposite of love is not hatred—but indifference.*
>
> —Elie Wiesel, author and Nobel Peace Prize winner

History is replete with examples of people following toxic leaders. (The name Adolf Hitler comes to mind.) It can happen in schools as readily as anywhere else.

If one bad apple can spoil the whole barrel, just think what can happen if the rotten apple is also the lead apple. You can have a bad culture with a good leader; but you can't have a good culture with a bad leader.

There are lots of ways to screw up a school culture. Naturally, unprincipled and incompetent administrators try them all. In her fascinating book *The Allure of Toxic Leaders*, Jean Lipman-Bluman (2006) identifies some of the most common tactics of toxic bosses in all fields, including

- Disregarding people's rights
- Playing on individual vulnerabilities and fears

- Trafficking in illusion
- Misrepresenting and misdiagnosing issues and problems
- Promoting incompetence, cynicism, cronyism, and even corruption

Toxic leaders are also notorious for meddling and micromanaging, either out of fear of losing control or of being left out of the loop, or out of a false sense of competence. Business columnist Dale Dauten calls this illusion of grandeur by pseudoleaders "cranial-rectal inversion" (the less they know, the more they think they know).

Micromanagement almost always has poisonous effects on the organization. My wife and I experienced this phenomenon firsthand a few years ago when we cochaired an important lay board in our church. Since, between us, we had chaired, conducted, and presided over hundreds of meetings, forums, committees, and task forces, we felt we had something to contribute and were excited about the opportunity; but our euphoria was short-lived.

For some reason, one of the paid church staff members felt compelled to sit in on all our meetings, watchdog our leadership, amend our agendas, question our actions, drop accusatory hints at omissions on our part, and subtly scold us for perceived shortcomings.

The board meetings became increasingly dreaded and dreadful. Eventually, the overattentive official micromanaged us into disillusionment. We gave up and couldn't wait until our term was over.

Does this kind of thing happen in schools? You bet. Does it happen in your school? Think twice before you answer. Regardless of where it occurs, micromanagement is a prime example of toxic leadership in action.

Inside and outside of school, all of us have observed lethal leadership that diminishes an organization. I recall one superintendent (happily, she was never my boss) who could have been the poster child for venomous management. She employed all of Lipman-Blumen's strategies and added a few original wrinkles of her own. She hid money, ignored contract requirements, gave out false information (better known as lying), practiced blatant favoritism, isolated and undercut out-of-favor administrators, and surrounded herself with inept assistants who made her look good by contrast.

She was an expert on how not to create an organizational culture that works for everyone. Instead, she created a culture that worked for no one, except herself. Fortunately, cultures are resilient, and this one healed quickly after her departure.

Sadly, this is just one of the toxic school leaders I've encountered during my career. There are more. And I'm not the only one who has observed a noxious principal or superintendent here and there along the way. How many have you known?

How do people like this end up in responsible power positions in public schools? Sometimes, the only explanation is that they look the part—they look like leaders—what some writers call the "Warren Harding effect."

But no matter how they got there, toxic leaders can drag down a school's culture in a hurry. Usually, however, leaders don't contaminate a culture all by themselves. They have help.

Every organization has some pockets of pessimism or networks of negativity embedded somewhere in its culture. Even the happy-go-lucky seven dwarfs had their Grumpy, and the well-meaning Whos in Whoville had their Grinch. I'm sure you know who the toxic people are in your school.

They are the naysayers and the crepe-hangers. They are finger-pointers, footdraggers, and faultfinders. They undermine plans for improvement and manipulate all those around them. They constantly complain about the status quo, while resisting change at the same time. These are the people who consistently get in the way, block progress, slow things down, and tie up people and resources. They're stumbling blocks.

These stumbling blocks put their own needs above the school's mission and goals. Their bag of tricks includes half-truths, bent truths, untruths, diversions, delays, character assassination, smoke screens, espionage, and sabotage. Left unchallenged, unattended, and unaddressed, they can alter the ethos of the school—perhaps for good.

The good news is that knowledge is power. With an understanding of what contributes to a deadly culture, you can detoxify your school's environment. Later chapters (see Chapters 8, 9, and 10) contain a profusion of suggestions for eliminating toxic elements and shaping a customized culture that benefits everyone. If you want some teasers, here are two giant steps to get you started: (1) pay attention to size, and (2) hire stepping-stones.

Size matters. Education works best when it is personal. Kids learn as individuals, not as a mass. That's why we continue to build obscenely large schools of 2,000–3,000 children and teenagers at our peril. Recent studies show that megasize high schools develop bureaucratic, impersonal patterns similar to those in the nation's largest corporations.

Fortunately, more and more school districts are looking for ways to break down large educational units into smaller "houses" or "schools-within-a-school." There's a reason why the Bill & Melinda Gates Foundation gives millions of dollars annually to create small high schools. Anything you can do to organize workable-size learning environments upgrades your school's culture.

Likewise, you do your school environment a favor by building your staff out of stepping-stones, instead of stumbling blocks. What good schools need are teachers and other staff members who promote the common good and strengthen the overall school. These are professionals who are relentlessly positive, upbeat, hopeful, supportive, encouraging, and empowering. They are willing to sacrifice a little and to delay personal gratification to do the next right thing for all concerned.

They do their share and are willing to compromise their self-interests (but not their principles) to make collective gains. They make time and take time to improve the school for everyone. They move things forward, support the weight of others, define a preferred path, and point the way in the right direction. That's why I call them stepping-stones.

The more of these culture builders you have on board, the better. Of course, school leaders seldom have the luxury of hand-picking an entire staff; but like good landscapers, they can add one stepping-stone at a time until it's done. This doesn't mean just hiring people who think as you do; but it does mean hiring people who care as much as you do.

How do you find them? My favorite school system operates on the premise that they can teach newcomers all they need for the job, except passion. No matter how brilliant, energetic, well-trained, and ambitious candidates may be, you can't teach them "heart." ("Don't waste your time trying to change ducks into eagles," writes motivational author John Rohn.) Look first for the passion. That's how you find the stepping-stones to a more positive school culture.

And that's why the most important question to ask of potential staff members is, "Why do you want to teach?" If you can't detect a genuine love of kids or a real desire to help people and make a difference, look elsewhere. You want people who want to teach because it's teaching, not because it's a job. These are the stepping-stones. All others are most likely stumbling blocks.

If you recruit, attract, hire, and retain the right people and place them in a teaching environment of manageable size, you've made it virtually impossible for your school to develop a toxic culture.

But how do you know if and when it's time to downsize your school? Or bring in fresh faces? Or tune the bagpipes? How do you gauge what kind of culture you have or you are getting into? Fortunately, there are lots of formal and informal ways to size up how well a school environment works for everyone. It's like crime scene investigator (CSI) school. The evidence is all around you. You just have to know how and where to look. Start by looking at Chapter 5.

5

Assessing the DNA of Your School's Culture

Character is the personality of the organization; it is the DNA of the organizational life form. It is the organization's character that makes it feel and act like itself.

—William Bridges, author of *The Character of Organizations* (2000)

Often, you can quickly figure out, sometimes within hours of being in a place, what the culture encourages, rewards and promotes.

—Louis V. Gerstner, former CEO IBM Corporation, author of *Who Says Elephants Can't Dance?* (2003)

———————— ❦ ————————

Alcoholics Anonymous urges all its members to "take a fearless, moral inventory" and to "continue to take personal inventory and, when you are wrong, promptly admit it." That's good advice for everyone. It's also a success secret for organizations, like schools, that want to create an environment that works for everyone.

Unfortunately, it's more difficult than it sounds. Cultures are elusive, ethereal, and will-o'-the-wispy. They can't be counted, weighed, measured, tallied, x-rayed, dissected, scrutinized under a microscope, subjected to chemical analysis, or even autopsied. As with vampires, when you hold a mirror up to a culture, no image appears. That makes assessing the DNA of your school culture like trying to lasso smoke or weigh a ghost. But if you want to keep your school at the top of its game, you have to do it—and the sooner, the better.

I "got" this point years ago when I was assigned as an educational "CSI agent" to investigate what went terribly wrong with the culture of a troubled elementary school. Complaints about mistreatment, rights violations, and cruel and insensitive punishment in the school had been surfacing for some time. Finally, allegations reached a crescendo. A grassroots citizens action group was formed and demanded that the school board clean house, including firing the principal.

As a stopgap measure, two central office administrators ("me and the other guy") were designated to investigate the situation thoroughly and report back to the board and the community with recommendations for remediation. Little did we know what we were getting into.

Under advice from legal counsel, we set up shop in a neutral site and invited all those with grievances or complaints related to the school to come interview with us in a confidential setting. We then interviewed all comers for eight to ten hours a day, six days a week, for several weeks. It was like holding open house for everyone who had ever felt shortchanged, mistreated, ignored, snubbed, underappreciated, violated, used, or abused by the school.

Like real professional investigators, we followed a strict protocol. Each person interviewed was duly sworn in. We asked predetermined, structured questions, and then left room for open-ended questions and responses. We took copious notes and tape-recorded all sessions as well.

As time went by, more and more self-proclaimed victims came out of the woodwork. Many interviews begat other interviews. We heard war stories spanning several decades involving discourtesy, disrespect, humiliation, harsh punishment, discrimination, harassment, bullying, and even sexual abuse.

Some grievances were directed toward persons long since gone or retired from the school. Some complaints were legitimate. Some were bizarre. Others were eye-opening. A few were eye-rubbing, and one or two were downright scary.

When grievants and complainants stopped coming to us, we went to the school and interviewed everyone willing to talk to us in the presence of a court reporter. It was a "no-stone-left-unturned" thing.

At long last, after several months, we wrapped up our inquiry, ordered preparation of a complete transcript of all interviews (which ran to hundreds of pages), and drafted our final report. Thus ended my short and stormy career as a detective.

Our findings and conclusions were simple and direct. We found that most of the complaints stemmed from misunderstandings and miscommunication (no surprise there). Most could be traced back not to the principal but to one very loyal, but empathy-challenged, "pit bull" secretary. As a feisty gatekeeper, she managed to alienate almost everyone by her misguided attempts to buffer, protect, and shield her boss (the principal) from any unpleasantness.

Once all the pent-up hostilities were vented and the secretary in question "retired," things at the school returned to normal. The principal went on to enjoy a successful career in that and other schools. Sadly, if only a thorough "inventory" of the school's culture had been conducted much earlier, a great deal of grief could have been averted.

From this experience, I derived six important take-home lessons:

1. Complaining is contagious (even though some complaints are tangential or irrelevant).

2. Some people just like to complain and jump at any chance to vent.

3. The school is an easy scapegoat for many individual shortcomings.

4. Complaints and grievances are not always what they seem.

5. Good communication avoids or resolves most complaints and is essential to any successful culture.

6. It's never too soon to evaluate the personality and character of your organization.

You probably knew all this stuff already; but if not, you're welcome to my hard-earned wisdom.

The point is that assessing your school's culture isn't just a nice, trendy thing to do; it's a leadership imperative. Anything less is a dereliction of duty. The problem is how to do it.

It's true that you can walk into, through, or around a school for only a short period and often get a good feel for the culture. But that works only if it's someone else's school. In your own school, you are too much a part of the culture to rely on just your sense or feeling for how well it's doing.

It's okay to trust your gut at times. But your gut is too biased to be an accurate gauge of the environment in which you are immersed every day. You need something more reliable. You're in luck. Help is available.

Anything as multifaceted as a school culture requires multiple measures. That's why the best school leaders use both formal, structured, and objective measuring instruments and informal, more subjective assessment tools to evaluate how well their school environment is working for everyone.

> *Trust your gut, it doesn't know how to lie.*
>
> —Elvis Presley

Although culture assessment isn't an exact science, there are some systematic, objective means of taking the pulse of an organization. Many schools have had success by hiring marketing

specialists or professional pollsters to conduct scientifically designed, sophisticated consumer satisfaction surveys. These are particularly helpful in preparation for a levy referendum or bond issue campaign. The results can be as close to scientific findings about your culture as you're ever going to get.

Other schools periodically bring in trained observers to hold focus groups and/or observe the school's operations and interactions with internal and external audiences (constituencies). The objectivity of a third party certainly beats the denial, tunnel vision, and paranoia of self-diagnosis.

Schools can also borrow a page from the business sector and bring in "corporate chaplains" to conduct "cultural audits" of the organization. Often, businesses use chaplains who are licensed but are not ordained ministers.

Their role is to interview employees and other stakeholders (e.g., students and parents) to assess the organization's shared values and core attributes. They look closely at the ethics and principles of the leaders and try to determine if the organization is living its principles. The goal is to identify ways to encourage and maintain positive values. This process is especially useful in periods of rapid growth to keep the organization honest, grounded, and focused and ensure alignment between principles (mission) and practices.

In addition to these assessment techniques, there are a number of pencil-and-paper appraisal instruments that can give you a better handle on how healthy your school environment really is. The following two examples are typical.

The Organizational Character Index (OCI)

The Organizational Character Index (OCI) was developed by internationally acclaimed speaker, writer, and business consultant William Bridges. This instrument involves rating the organization in 36 areas (see sample items) and yields an overall numerical rating or score. The index is most reliable if completed by several raters inside, outside, and on different levels of the organization (e.g., teachers, administrators, board members, parents, and kids). For more information, check out *The Character of Organizations* by Bridges and published by Davies-Black Publishers.

OCI: Sample Items

	Efficiency		Effectiveness	
What is most important—efficiency or effectiveness?	1	2	3	4
	Actualities		*Possibilities*	
Guided by actualities of possibilities?	1	2	3	4

Assessing Your Role as Cultural Leader (Resource B)

Assessing Your Role as Cultural Leader (Resource B) is a copyrighted survey published in *What Every Principal Should Know About Cultural Leadership* (Corwin Press) by Jeffrey Glanz. This survey instrument rates the school's culture in several areas (see sample items) on a scale from Strongly Agree (SA) to Strongly Disagree (SD).

Resource B: Sample Items

Teachers are aware of the school's mission and goals.	SA	A	D	SD
Students are involved in decision making.	SA	A	D	SD

Of course, sometimes the best measuring stick for inventorying your school culture is a custom-made survey instrument you and your staff develop exclusively for your specific situation. This is the only way to be sure you ask the questions you want to ask and not just questions someone else thinks you should ask. And it's easier than you may think. See the sample Morale Survey I helped develop several years ago for a suburban school district in Minnesota.

These examples of available survey instruments demonstrate that there are formal tools for evaluating school environments. None of these instruments is perfect. They can be misused. The greatest misuse is not to use any method of examining the health—strengths and weaknesses (there will always be weaknesses)—of your organization. As a school leader, you don't get to do nothing.

Cultural assessment is a little like soil sampling. Each measuring tool can give you insight into certain aspects of your school environment. The best approach is to take several borings (samples) from as many different areas as possible. Not all these borings have to be scientific samples. Some can be just informal observations.

Don't pooh-pooh informal indicators of cultural performance just because they are unscientific. They provide unique personal "peepholes" into the internal life of the school that you wouldn't have otherwise. Sometimes a little objective observation can give you more insight and information than a dozen surveys can reveal.

The keys to informal assessment of the school culture are *intention* and *attention*—consciously noticing what's really going on all around you every day. The trick is to know where to look, how to look, what to look for, and what questions to ask while you're looking.

Model Morale Survey (Abridged)

How to Complete the Survey

There are no right or wrong answers. All we want is your personal opinion based on your knowledge and experience. Stay anonymous.

Key

SA = Strongly Agree

TA = Tend to Agree

TD = Tend to Disagree

SD = Strongly Disagree

Circle the Answer That Best Fits Your Opinion

1. The district administration's decisions seem fair.	SA	TA	TD	SD
2. In general, I approve of district policy.	SA	TA	TD	SD
3. I have little opportunity to express my ideas to administration.	SA	TA	TD	SD
4. I am treated like a professional at all times.	SA	TA	TD	SD
5. I am rarely told whether or not I am doing good work.	SA	TA	TD	SD
6. There is too much friction between professional and nonprofessional staff.	SA	TA	TD	SD
7. My supervisor is responsive to my needs.	SA	TA	TD	SD
8. Administration does a good job of responding to complaints.	SA	TA	TD	SD
9. My supervisor shows initiative in seeking ways to help us in our work.	SA	TA	TD	SD
10. The district's rules make sense to me.	SA	TA	TD	SD
11. My performance is judged fairly.	SA	TA	TD	SD
12. Administration does all it can to build an effective program.	SA	TA	TD	SD
13. My principal tries to get my ideas.	SA	TA	TD	SD
14. We are kept well informed of matters affecting our work.	SA	TA	TD	SD
15. It is often difficult to get the assistance I need.	SA	TA	TD	SD
16. My performance appraisals help me to improve my work	SA	TA	TD	SD

Evidence about your school's environment is everywhere. If you are like many principals and superintendents, however, you are not in the habit of really seeing what you are looking at.

So where do you look to find the vital signs of your school's culture? Where are the clues that can tell you how well the culture is working for everyone? Try stepping back and taking a second long, hard look at pieces of evidence right under your nose, such as

Attendance records (for both students and staff)

Awards received

Contract negotiations sticking points

Course selection patterns

Discipline records

External rankings and ratings

Grievances filed

Informal memos and correspondence

Minutes of meetings

Performance appraisals

Police calls to the school

Policy statements

Questions received from the public

Referrals

Substitute teacher records

Telephone logs

Transfers (of both students and staff)

Turnout figures for open houses and parent conferences

Volunteer records

And pay special attention to

- *Test Scores (standardized tests, graduation standards measures, college entrance exams).* Take particular notice of performance gaps between majority and minority students.
- *Budgets.* Where the money is spent speaks volumes about the real priorities of the school.
- *Buildings and Grounds.* These are the face of the culture. Excessive litter, graffiti, and vandalism are all signs of a toxic culture.
- *Media Reports, Editorials, and Letters to the Editor.* Even negative coverage can be instructive. After all, enemies of the school will tell you what's wrong, while friends may sugarcoat bad news. The media is the voice of the community on school matters. It reflects community concerns and shapes public perception and opinion at the same time.
- And most important, look at the faces of the children entering and leaving the school, passing in the halls, and in the classrooms. Their faces and posture can tell you more than a plethora of focus groups.

If there is joy and hope in the school, it will show. If there is fear and despair, it will show as well. While you're at it, also study the faces of teachers and others who work in the school. Faces can tell you a lot about what it's like to work and learn in your school.

Obviously, there is ample available evidence to detect what's going on in your school culture. But how should you look for it? How do you gather it? How do you find the clues that tell you what condition the culture is in? You simply use the same six investigative tools that the best leaders in all fields employ, including:

1. SOLICIT FEEDBACK AND INPUT

Set up online suggestion boxes. Conduct your own surveys, polls, focus groups, and exit interviews. (Sometimes, a show of hands can be an adequate polling device.) Sit down one-on-one with the people you trust—and even some you don't trust all that much—and pick their brains on what is right and wrong about your school. Schedule a "youth summit" where students can talk freely about how it feels to be a kid in your school, while the adults just listen, without intervening or interrupting.

In short, scrounge, scrape, and scrap for any shred of evidence that can give you a better glimpse of the real climate in your school.

2. GO WHERE THE ACTION IS

"Management While Walking Around" (MWWA) isn't just a management mantra. It should be the way you do business every day.

Don't wait for evidence of your culture's health or toxicity to come to you or magically appear on your desk. Go find it. Go to where things are happening, including "ground zero" of every crisis. Good leaders "live in the village."

3. OBSERVE EARLY AND OFTEN

Keep your eyes open. Visit classes. Spend time in the teachers' lounge. Ride a school bus. Sit in on committee meetings and parent meetings. Attend social events, student activities, and sporting contests.

Don't just show up, make an appearance, or spend all your time watching the scoreboard. Study the dynamics of interaction. Notice who people listen to and why. Try to detect how intense, comfortable, or confrontational students and staff members seem to be. Pay attention to how problems are faced and solved (or not). See whether or not people are having fun. (For example, how much do people laugh in meetings?) Seeing is believing. What you see is what you've got.

4. LISTEN MORE, TALK LESS

Eavesdrop if you have to. Hear what people are saying when their guard is down. Listen to the feelings behind the words. Notice the metaphors people use to describe what goes on in your school. (Too many military comparisons should be a red flag.) You can tell a lot about an organization by the way it talks about itself.

5. ASK PEOPLE DIRECTLY WHAT THEY THINK AND FEEL ABOUT THE ORGANIZATION

Question students, teachers, and parents. Don't let them squirm out of answering. And make a special effort to ask

- *Custodians.* They know what's used, abused, and wasted in the school. They know, better than anyone, the incidents of vandalism. They know who the best and worst teachers are. They know the gossip. And they know the truth. Custodians know pretty much everything about the school.
- *School Bus Drivers.* They hear it all—the good, the bad, and the ugly. And they usually don't mind repeating it.
- *Substitute Teachers.* Nobody has a better basis for comparison. Substitutes see the school at its worst. And they have no vested interest or special loyalty. They tell it like it is.
- *Realtors.* They know what the scuttlebutt about the school is out in the community. And as it turns out, the scuttlebutt is often right.

6. TRY TO SEE THE SCHOOL THROUGH THE EYES OF OTHERS

One way is to call the school anonymously and see how the school secretary or receptionist responds to tough questions. It can give you an unrehearsed look at part of the climate in the school. (Remember the overzealous "pit bull" secretary who tried too hard to shelter her boss.)

Also try talking to former students further up the food chain in the educational system. They know how your culture stacks up against other schools.

Of course, none of these investigative techniques works unless you pay close attention, practice active listening, and repeatedly ask yourself, "What's really going on here?"

———— ✄ ————

Get the facts, or the facts will get you. And when you get them, get them right or they will get you wrong.

—Dr. Thomas Fuller (1654–1734)

Look for trends, patterns, and unexpected blips on the radar screen. Be sure you have your facts straight and that your observations are accurate.

Even though they are imperfect and require extra work, informal (unscientific) assessments, like those above, are essential components in any inventory of organizational culture. If you want to find out what really makes your school tick—what's behind the lofty slogans, polished terrazzo, slick brochures, and pollyannic handbooks—you need to do a little snooping on your own. It pays to add some unorthodox dimensions to your fact-finding.

Admittedly, there is no foolproof way for you to learn everything about your school's culture; but making the extra effort to tap into atypical sources and to try some novel approaches can get you a lot closer.

Naturally, looking in all the right places, in all the right ways, won't be useful unless you know what you are looking for. What are the signs that your culture is on the right track?

Following are examples of the types of evidence you want to find when examining the character of your school. (If you don't find these or similar evidence of good health, it may be time to visit the "culture doctor.")

Evidence of a Positive School Culture

- Substitutes request to work in your building.
- People show up in your office with offers to help, not just with problems and complaints.
- Former students return to teach in your school.
- Both students and staff have good attendance records—especially on Mondays and Fridays.
- People seem generally happy and satisfied.
- There are no significant incidents of racial flare-ups, violence, harassment, or bullying.
- Strangers seem to feel welcome.
- You hear the words "we," "us," and "ours" frequently.
- Conversations are respectful.
- Teachers don't automatically shut up when an administrator enters the room.

- Students are willing to ask questions, seek help, and share their finished work with pride.
- There is not an excess of "A" grades, but not many students fail either.
- There is high participation in academic extracurricular activities (e.g., debate, quiz bowl, math team) as well as in athletics.
- There is evidence of positive responses to problems and crises. (One of the best examples I know of occurred at Rocori High School in Minnesota, which was devastated when a school shooter—a student in the school—killed two of his classmates. But one year later, on the anniversary of the tragedy, the entire school joined in a "Celebration of Life" by attaching positive messages to helium-filled balloons and releasing them en masse. Resilience, buoyed by hope, like that at Rocori High is a definite indicator of a strong, positive organizational character.)

The more of these or similar positive indicators you find in your school, the better. Don't be surprised if you uncover some warts and blemishes as well. Hopefully, you will find more crinkles (from laughter) than wrinkles (from frowning).

Throughout the inventory process, whatever tools and techniques you use will yield more meaningful results if you know the right questions to ask. Whether dealing with individuals or groups, with students or staff, with parents or other community members, questions, like the following, cut to the core of your culture:

- What are you most proud of about the school?
- What are your dreams for the school? Your worst nightmare?
- What are you afraid of about the school's future?
- If you could send your children to any school, would you enroll them here? Why or why not?
- What are you ashamed of or embarrassed by in our school?
- As a stakeholder in the school, what do you regret most?
- What is an annual highlight for you in the school?
- If we were to bury a time capsule of things representing our school, what should we put in it?
- If you could change just one thing about our school, what would it be? Why?
- What three words best describe our school through the students' eyes? The staff's perspective? The parents' viewpoints?

If you can get honest answers to these questions from all those involved, you will have a clear, well-rounded picture of whether or not your school climate benefits everyone.

Taking this kind of inventory of your organizational culture is not easy, and it's not always fun, but it is always worthwhile. Best of all, it has one unexpected side effect.

The mere act of initiating the inventory itself can boost your culture. There is an old saying in business, "People respect what you inspect." It's true in schools as well.

————————— ✂ —————————

. . . no credit can be given for predicting rain—only for building arks.

—Louis V. Gerstner, former CEO IBM Corporation, author of *Who Says Elephants Can't Dance?* (2003)

Simply by asking, "How are we doing?" and "How can we do better?" you send a message that the climate and feeling tone of the school are important and that you care about them. This alone is enough to cause some people to do better and be better. There aren't many bonuses in this business. This is one of them!

When all the evidence is in and the assessment of the school's DNA is complete, the only remaining questions are, "So what?" and "What next?" Then, the fun begins.

As leader, you now have some judgment calls to make, because the inventory makes a difference only if you act on the results.

If taking your school's temperature does nothing more than renew efforts to get healthy and stay healthy as a culture, it is worthwhile. If it keeps the organization from shooting itself in the foot, that's even better. Chapter 6 explains why.

6

Avoiding "Fratricide"

(Death by Friendly Fire)

We have met the enemy and he is us.

—Pogo, comic strip character created
by Walt Kelly

*Most barriers to success are man-made. And most often, you're the
man who made them.*

—Frank Tyger, writer

———————————— ✢ ————————————

"Fratricide" is a euphemistic term the Pentagon sometimes uses to describe death by friendly fire—being killed not by the enemy but accidentally by your own side. A lot of this goes on in wartime, I guess. But that's not the only situation where friendly fire occurs. It happens a lot with school cultures as well.

Schools are frequently under attack. Yet school cultures are seldom brought down by enemy fire. They are much more likely to be diminished, damaged, or destroyed by their own kind, or to self-destruct. They implode a lot.

Good cultures that go bad often suffer from internal decay. They tend to rot from the inside out. You don't want to let that happen on your watch. You don't want any part of deadly friendly fire.

There is a reason this book is titled *Don't Teach the Canaries Not to Sing.* Remember the Hippocratic Oath? As principal or superintendent, your first responsibility is to do no harm. Don't let the culture self-mutilate, collapse under its own weight, or turn sour by deed or default. It's your job to protect the school environment and avoid fratricide.

Likewise, don't let anyone, inside or outside of the organization—including yourself—contaminate the culture. Even if you have to fire your own boss.

Well, that may be a bit too extreme; but I did know a high school principal who once ordered a district office supervisor of "home economics" out of his school for good.

In this case, the principal objected to the supervisor's effort to block the path his staff wanted to take and felt she threatened the cohesion of his team. So he "fired" her. Would you go that far? Maybe not—but it underscores the importance of protecting the school culture.

The remainder of this book is crammed with credible strategies for avoiding dry rot or self-inflicted wounds and for building a world-class school climate that is healthy for everyone. For now, the first step is to grasp the most common causes of cultural collapse from the inside out.

Bad things happen to good cultures, and no school environment is entirely pure and unpolluted. This isn't always a bad thing, because a little imperfection makes the culture more interesting. When enough bad things infiltrate the milieu of the school, however, the culture becomes dysfunctional. Some of the most harmful contaminants that people frequently bring into or allow to develop inside the school environment include:

NEGATIVE TALK (HARMFUL CONVERSATIONS)

This includes vicious gossip, rumor-mongering, name-calling, labeling, and libeling. Bad-mouthing is a communicable disease. It's contagious. It impairs collaboration, promotes suspicion, creates division, isolates stakeholders, fosters resentment, and establishes a judgmental, punitive atmosphere.

Good communication is healthy. But this kind of bitter chatter is dangerous. I almost said it is evil—I will say it—it's actually evil.

BUREAUCRACY AND RED TAPE

A bureaucracy is its own worst enemy. Cultures can be "trifled" to death by endless reporting, record keeping, approvals, forms, files, channels, committees, meetings, obstacles, and roadblocks. Jumping through hoops is not healthy exercise for any organization.

Bureaucracy impersonalizes and dehumanizes the culture, marginalizes the people in it, squelches creativity, and makes teaching and learning boring drudgery. How is that good for any culture? The flatter and leaner the organization, the healthier the culture. After all, a flat organization can't collapse.

CLIQUES AND FACTIONS

Every culture has subcultures. But when the lines between cliques and factions harden and the subgroups actively work against each other, everyone suffers.

When subcultures become hurtful to each other, they fragment the organization. Subgroups can subvert the entire culture. It's okay to have cliques; but the cliques have to click or the culture unravels.

"US" VERSUS "THEM" MENTALITY

Excessive competition, rivalries, and turf battles divide and polarize the culture and pit departments, grade levels, or entire schools against each other.

Administrators often generate some of this friendly fire by placing too much emphasis on comparing test scores. Friendly competition can motivate and boost productivity; but unhealthy competition can become the friendly fire that mortally wounds the culture.

BLAMING AND SHAMING

When excuse making becomes an integral part of the culture, any semblance of cooperation, teamwork, or accountability goes out the window. Find a culture riddled with finger-pointing and you will find a culture pointed in the wrong direction.

SECRETS AND LIES

If trust and honesty are the life's blood of successful organizations and healthy cultures, secrets and lies are deadly infections. No sound culture can be built on falsehoods. It's too weak a foundation.

When the school is less than truthful with parents or the public, or when the administration purposely misrepresents situations to the faculty or student body, the culture becomes dangerously polluted.

Fortunately, this is one thing you can do something about. Value the truth. Model it. Insist on it. The truth may cause temporary pain, discomfort, or embarrassment—but it will eventually set you free and allow the culture to meet everybody's needs.

ISOLATION

The antithesis of culture is isolation. When teachers work in isolation and administration distances itself from staff and students, there is no culture, no sense of community, and no common cause. That's why a large measure of culture building is breaking down barriers and removing obstacles.

UNREALISTIC EXPECTATIONS

Denial takes many forms. One is false expectations. When the expectations for students or teachers are unrealistically high, the culture is on a collision course with calamity. Unrealistic hopes and standards only set everyone up for disappointment and failure. Cultures need dreams, not pie-in-the-sky illusions.

At first, each of these impurities may seem innocent and innocuous. Left alone, like cancer cells, they insidiously infest and infect the larger body. Singly or in combination, they can poison the atmosphere, making it unfit for productive teaching and learning.

FEAR AND DISTRUST

Unfortunately, the aforementioned are not the greatest internal threats to the culture. The two deadliest causes of fratricide in schools are *fear* and *distrust*.

Fear is a crippler. It has no place in any school. It paralyzes, polarizes, and pulverizes the culture quicker than any other single factor.

I'm reminded of a friend who, on the eve of a benchmark birthday, suddenly suffered severe chest pains and shortness of breath and began to sweat profusely. Naturally, he was rushed to the ER and immediately hospitalized.

The next day, after exhausting the clinic's repertoire of tests, he emerged with a clean bill of health. The doctors could find nothing wrong with him. What happened?

My friend later figured it out. No one else in his family had ever lived to the age he was about to celebrate. Subconsciously, he feared his own death and literally scared himself into a faux heart attack.

If fear can do this to an individual, just think what it can do to an entire organization. It bears repeating—fear has no place in your school.

Distrust is the second deadliest pollutant that can poison the school atmosphere. (Actually, fear and distrust are virtually inseparable. It's difficult to rank one over the other.) But distrust is a deal breaker. It not only negates any other positive attributes of the culture but also defines and becomes the culture.

In *Creating a Positive School Culture,* authors Marie-Nathalie Beaudoin and Maureen Taylor write about the "cycle of distrust" that can wreck any culture in a hurry. As adults in the school (or in the community) distrust, suspect, and fear young people (their students), the students begin to distrust, suspect, and fear the adults. And the cycle begins. Distrust on one side begets distrust on the other side.

The cycle can only widen and deepen and become a self-fulfilling prophecy. This cycle is not just a never-ending circle; it is a downward spiral descending into cultural oblivion.

And the cycle of distrust doesn't just threaten the adult-student relationships; it can infect teacher-administrator relationships, teacher-parent relationships, school-community relationships, and all the other intertwining relationships that make up the web of the culture. Distrust is obviously a menace you want to keep out of your school at all costs.

When fear and distrust pollute the climate of any school, even the Environmental Protection Agency can't help much. As leader, if you do anything to cause or allow these deadly infestations to become part of the school environment, you are actually pulling the trigger on friendly fire that can wipe out the school's culture. That's not a legacy you want to leave.

From a leader's view, the greatest problem with fratricide in schools is that it can target any component of the culture. The basic premise of this book is that in order to work, the school culture must work for all groups involved. If the culture fails any of the stakeholders, it fails them all, and it fails itself. Unfortunately, it is not difficult for the culture to unintentionally shortchange one or more of the partners.

The culture fails the students whenever it does anything to impersonalize education (treat kids as cogs), to treat all students the same (how many times have we responded to diversity with standardization?), or to trap or entrap them.

I once saw a test item that asked students to name the only woman who knew the true identity of the Lone Ranger. Who knows such a thing? (Incidentally, the answer is Clara Hornblower.) Who cares? What difference does it make? Asking stupid stuff is entrapment. It's easy for the culture to fail the pupils. It happens somewhere every day.

> *Teaching is the downstairs maid of professions. Teachers are told to use the service door or to go around to the back.*
>
> —Frank McCourt, author of *Teacher Man* (2006)

And the culture fails the staff whenever it restrains and constrains them with bureaucratic locks and chains, or treats them as less than valued professionals. It's easy for the culture to fail the staff. In many places, it's the norm.

Likewise, the culture fails the parents whenever it assumes that the school knows more about their own children than they do or excludes

them from decision making about their children's education or makes false promises to them and their kids (e.g., inflated grades). It's easy for the school culture to fail the parents. You've probably been a party to it. So have I.

And the culture fails the community members whenever it keeps secrets from them or treats the community like an ATM by going to them only when it needs more money or talks down to them in a secret language all its own (e.g., "In reporting test results, the analysis of variance is a statistical procedure for resolving the total variance of a set of varieties into component variances that are associated with various factors affecting the varieties . . ." Huh?). It's easy for the school culture to fail the community. It's stupid and shortsighted, but it happens with some regularity.

The point is that fratricide can attack any or all of the components that make up the school culture. When it does, the principal or superintendent usually gets the blame—and often, they deserve it.

Through ignorance, arrogance, innocence, naïveté, vanity, false pride, egotism, insecurity, malicious intent, or old-fashioned incompetence, school leaders frequently do a lot of moronic or mischievous things that come back to haunt them and harm the school environment.

A few blatantly ambitious administrators simply don't care what damage they do to the culture, as long as they advance their careers. For them, the position of principal or superintendent isn't a destination, but merely a stepping-stone. Such pseudoleaders don't deserve the trust the community has placed in them.

As Bill George, former CEO of Medtronic, Inc., explains, "One of the greatest obstacles to teacher satisfaction and performance is a leader's drive for status and power. Career lust is almost always a culture killer." When leaders indulge themselves with lavish perks and the trappings of power, they are damaging their standing and leadership.

Executive leadership is not slash-and-burn farming—the mining of the institutional soil and then moving to the next field to be harvested.

—Charles M. Denny, CEO
ADT Telecommunications, Inc.

Sometimes, leaders do violence to the school culture through outrageous acts, such as the Alabama high school principal who threatened to cancel the 1994 prom to prevent interracial couples from attending. Later that night, the school was the victim of arson. Talk about friendly fire! With a leader like that, the culture doesn't need any other enemies.

Usually, however, school officials practice fratricide in more subtle ways. For example, I've known a superintendent who excluded out-of-favor administrators from important meetings and didn't even talk to her assistant superintendent for the first several months on the job, and a superintendent who didn't want to waste time socializing with his own office staff.

I've known a principal who hid in the backseat of his car during much of the school day, and another principal who hid in the closet when irate parents appeared at the school, leaving his secretary to deal with the parental hostility. All these "leaders" were major contributors to a toxic culture within their organization. You can probably think of even worse examples from your own experience.

Pogo was right: often, the enemy is us. Thanks to impulsive decision making, lack of vision, refusal to delegate, unilateral actions, shortsighted choices, uncompromising behavior, stonewalling, nit-picking, impatience, immaturity, or underdeveloped interpersonal skills, many school leaders unwittingly undermine the very culture they are trying to build. You don't want to be one of them. You don't want to give the orders that initiate hazardous friendly fire. And you definitely don't want to be the one who pulls the trigger.

Good news. You don't have to be. Fratricide is always a danger, but it is not inevitable. You can learn how to help your school culture avoid death (or even minor injury) by friendly fire. This book can help.

How can you protect the culture from self-destructive influences? For starters, by taking the same measures that military commanders often employ to limit lethal friendly fire in combat:

- Identify targets (goals) well in advance.
- Have a plan and stick to it.
- Keep all the key players in the loop (and on the same page).
- Maintain a free flow of up-to-date information in all directions throughout the organization. (Be sure the left hand knows what the right hand is doing.)
- Have a predetermined contingency plan.
- Look twice before taking action.
- Resist knee-jerk reaction.

If it works for the Defense Department, it just may be useful in your school as well; but it's not enough.

Effective leaders do much more to avoid fostering attitudes or actions that feed the enemy within and, at the same time, resist external forces that can weaken the culture from the outside.

It probably doesn't say anywhere in your job description that you are the defender, protector, and chief caretaker of the school climate—but it should.

Of course, school leaders don't single-handedly forge the organization's culture. Sometimes, the culture evolves even in spite of them; but just as a teacher pretty much sets the classroom climate, the principal or superintendent plays a prominent role in shaping the culture of the entire school or district. Chapter 7 explains exactly what that role is, and how to play it like the best in the business do.

7

A Dresser of Sycamore Trees

The Leader's Role in Shaping the School's Culture

The leader must create the conditions for change in the culture.

—Louis V. Gerstner, former CEO
IBM Corporation, author of *Who Says
Elephants Can't Dance?* (2003)

The only power the principal really has is that of creating a context where everybody, students and adults, can be at their best.

—Marie-Nathalie Beaudoin and Maureen Taylor
authors of *Creating a Positive
School Culture* (2004)

———————— ✀ ————————

I'm not going all religious on you, but are you familiar with the story of the Biblical prophet Amos? Although he was recognized as a prophet, Amos was a humble man who worked at pinching the fruit of sycamore trees to soften it up enough so poor people could eat it. He even called himself a "dresser of sycamore trees." The sycamore was commonly considered the "poor man's fig tree." Amos possessed great humility and a deep commitment to selfless service. He was both a leader and a servant at the same time. Does that remind you of anything? It should.

Because more and more effective leaders, in all fields—especially in schools—are becoming practitioners of servant leadership. The idea is that the leader serves the organization, rather than controlling it. Leadership, then, exists for the benefit of the followers, and humility is its core.

———— ✂ ————

As a manager, it's not about you.

—Jack Welch, former CEO of GE

Of course, this is not a new idea. The Bible is full of references to servant leaders such as Amos—including Jesus. And it's not just the Bible speaking. (The Ojibwa tribes also preach that a leader puts the needs of the people first.)

There may not be many aspects of school administration that are inspired by Biblical examples, but this is one of them. I'm not suggesting that you wash the feet of your followers; but if you want a positive, fully functioning culture in your school, you need a servant's heart (e.g., accepting, unselfish, caring, and empathetic).

For culture building, servant leadership is "in." The days of being an all-autonomous, rock-'em-sock-'em boss are over. It doesn't work anymore—if it ever did.

What works now is finding ways to remove obstacles and help all partners and participants of the organization to perform and contribute to their maximum potential. Thus, the leader's role in shaping the school culture is primarily to serve the needs of all stakeholders. Sound tricky? Complicated? Challenging?

It is all of the above. But it is also satisfying, rewarding, and the most fun you can have and still call it "work." Look around at the most successful principals and superintendents in your area. They're not bullies or drill sergeants. They're not pencil-pushing bureaucrats either. They're servant leaders. You need to be one, too.

One of the best examples of a true servant leader I've ever known was Harold Enestvedt. "Mr. Enestvedt," as he was popularly called, presided over a suburban school district that experienced rapid, explosive, and exponential growth year after year for more than two decades. New schools and new attendance areas were an annual event. Teachers were frequently shuffled around, and many students attended a different school every year.

But through all the tumult and upheaval, the district managed to build and sustain a culture known for its loyalty, pride, and peak performances. Teachers and parents continued to be attracted to the district and continued to buy into the culture.

Much of the culture's strength was derived from Mr. Enestvedt's commitment to children, old-fashioned work ethic, and unequivocal integrity. Much of his character was reflected in the advice he gave to fellow educators:

- Work hard.
- Be honest.
- Be humble.
- Tell people you love them.

It's a philosophy that is difficult to improve upon.

Likewise, his compassion was evidenced by the fact that he replayed the tape of his wife's memorial service once a month for 14 years after her death. With that capacity for love, it's no surprise that Mr. Enestvedt was universally respected throughout the community.

The legacy of Harold Enestvedt's low-key leadership was a climate of quality teaching and learning that has carried forward to this day. He was superintendent of the St. Louis Park, Minnesota, public schools for 24 years. In the succeeding 24 years, the district had six more superintendents. Nationwide, the average tenure of superintendents today is about three years. Maybe they don't make culture builders like they used to.

Mr. Enestvedt was the kind of leader he was largely because of the self-disciplined Scandinavian culture in which he grew up. That's the way it works. People create a culture, and then it shapes them.

But for whatever reason, Enestvedt was the consummate servant leader. Of course, he didn't create a "lighthouse" school culture all by himself—but he was the preeminent contributor. That's the way it can be with you and your school culture as well.

Naturally, there are many things that even the best servant leaders can't do. No matter how good they are, administrators cannot script the school culture—or mandate, prescribe, impose, force, command, or demand a predetermined environment in the school—or create it by executive edict, or build it single-handedly, or will it into existence. What can a principal or superintendent do to "grow" a culture that works for everyone?

The answer is—more than you can measure. Despite all the limitations, the scary part is that the kind of culture your school has is still largely your fault (or to your credit). Although you can't dictate the culture, you can strongly influence it and nudge it in the direction of the mission by what you say, do, model, pay attention to, praise, recognize, reinforce, reward, applaud,laugh at, question, ignore, make public pronouncements about, or include in your priorities.

In short, everything you do or say—including memos, e-mails, offhand comments, and the jokes you tell—helps sculpt the culture of the organization. More than anything else, the climate of the school is the creation of the leader. Like it or not, you are a culture builder—sometimes, by default.

Of course, some aspects of the organizational culture develop naturally, randomly, unattended, and unintended; but much of it is planted or planned. To be a successful school leader today, you have to take the role of culture builder seriously because a positive culture makes good things happen.

An effective school has to be more than a place where happy people have fun working comfortably together. It also has to produce results. Fortunately, these two scenarios are not mutually exclusive. In fact, they support each other. The best results (e.g., test scores, graduation rates, and so on) come from schools with a culture that helps people produce, as well as to feel accepted, valued, recognized, and rewarded. That's why wise principals and superintendents invest time, energy, and effort in caring for the culture. It pays off in improved performance.

It should come as no surprise, however, that this servant leadership and culture building entail some new wrinkles—a new form of management and stewardship.

Traditionally, school administrators have been largely troubleshooters, problem solvers, and institutional repairpersons. Typically, they have found out what's not working and fixed it—but just fixing what's broken isn't enough anymore.

Too many school leaders spend too much time putting out fires and applying splints and Band-Aids—and not enough time building on strengths and helping a good culture get better.

If you like metaphors, it is no secret that patched-up tires don't always run smoothly or last very long. Neither do patched-up organizations.

For servant leaders, pinpointing problems and coming up with remedies aren't enough. Instead, they focus even more on enhancing and expanding what's already working just fine. No school can move from good to great merely by healing wounds. If school leaders ask questions only about what's not working and how to fix it, the school becomes a patchwork quilt of remedies and is defined only by its weaknesses.

To succeed as a servant leader today, principals and superintendents have to be more than a "Mr. or Ms. Fix-it." They also have to "fix" on strengthening and improving what's right within the organization. With this in mind, what exactly is the leader's role in creating a positive school culture? The best I can do is share the most precise job description for culture builders that I know of.

Leaders' Responsibilities for Culture Building

- Read the culture.
- Define the culture.
- Articulate the culture.

- Defend the culture.
- Celebrate the culture.
- Study the history and anthropology of the culture.
- Assess, respect, and enforce core values.
- Focus on and strengthen existing values.
- Renew the energy of the vision.
- Build on existing traditions.
- Reaffirm values through behaviors and routines.
- Develop new rituals, traditions, and ceremonies that fit the culture.
- Protect, create, encourage, and refine symbols of the culture[a] (see note below).
- Challenge traditions that no longer fit the culture[b] (see note below).
- Serve as conscience of the organization.
- Actively try to align the culture with the mission[c] (see note below).
- Create a new dream.
- Be a healer (oversee and smooth out transitions).
- Do everything else (that is not illegal, immoral, unethical, unprofessional, or injurious to health and safety) to build the hands-down best school culture in the world.
- Set examples.
- Share success stories.
- Build consensus.
- Strengthen linkages.
- Be a senior adviser.

a. The power of symbols was brought to my attention again recently when I learned that officials at my alma mater, the University of Kansas, were removing the well-known "Jayhawk" figure from all letterheads and business cards. The Jayhawk was viewed as frivolous and ill-suited to represent an academic institution. Along with others, I challenged the decision as being "stupid, stuffy, and humorless" and ignoring the power of one of the world's most recognized symbols. I didn't prevail on this issue, but I still think I was right. In reforming the symbol, the powers that be sacrificed an important piece of the culture.

b. A good example is the time-honored tradition of school prom. Once a valued rite of passage for all students, the event has become an elitist, ostentatious affair costing families hundreds—if not thousands—of dollars for fancy clothes, expensive dinners, flowers, limousines, hotel rooms, and more. Many middle- and lower-class kids can no longer afford to attend prom. It is now divisive and discriminatory. Besides, it contributes to the deaths of numerous teenage drivers each year. Is this a legitimate tradition that fits the culture of the "public" schools? I don't think so. If I had my way, prom would be replaced by a more informal, low-key, and less expensive celebration open equally to all kids. End of sermon.

c. Like a potter working with clay, school leaders often have to "center" the organization before they can shape it into new forms.

That's the job. That's what culture building is all about. Are you up to the task? If you are gainfully employed as a school administrator and interested enough to read this far in this book, you probably have what it takes.

But if you'd like a checklist to follow, below are the traits most likely to help you to succeed as an effective servant leader and to foster a positive school climate. Of course, not many school leaders possess all these qualities, but the best principals and superintendents have most of them.

Servant Leadership Traits

———————— ❧ ————————

What we need is love without getting tired.

—Mother Teresa

Whether you're a gazelle or a lion, you have to wake up running.

—Keith Greer
marketing specialist

A good sense of humor helps to overlook the unbecoming, understand the unconventional, tolerate the unpleasant, overcome the unexpected, and outlast the unbearable.

—Harvey Mackay, CEO, author, and motivational speaker

You don't just need to know where the rocks are; but where the rocks are not as well.

—Advice from unknown fishing guide

- Passion
- Strong moral compass
- Trustworthiness/credibility
- Nonjudgmental attitude
- A beginner's eye (ability to look at things with a fresh perspective as if seeing them for the first time)

And my personal favorite traits:

- Boldness. Culture building requires a modicum of courage, confidence, and cockiness to take risks, try new things, push the envelope, and stretch the organization. Patricia Harvey, a former superintendent, may have expressed it best: "I want to slay dragons. I want to do the most aggressive work we can do in public education." How's that for a leadership mantra?
- Quick thinking/quick action
- Humor. If you can't spot the silliness in some of our inevitable "stupid educator tricks," laugh with others, and laugh at yourself, you're probably not going to last. If you do last, you won't be very happy.
- Patience

> - Cultures, like glaciers, move in their own time. Change is a slow, multi-stage process. The best advice is to go slow, start small, do what you can to affect your own sphere for the good, and know how to practice the "difficult art of orderly retreat." The worst mistake you can make is to take on embedded values that are considered sacred within the culture. Good leaders know when to push and when to wait.

It would be nice if all there was to creating a positive culture was simply applying the talents and traits above to the tasks in the job description, but there's more to it than that—much more.

There is a whole creative process of assessment, education, judgment, initiative, coordination, motivation, timing, politics, adaptation, adjustment, refinement, and finesse. A process filled with delicate distinctions, nuances, and subtleties. It's called leadership.

It begins with establishing trust by listening to all the voices, treating everyone as an insider, giving credit, keeping your word, and spending praise generously. (For example, an old mentor once advised me to end every project and activity by expressing "lavish praise and heartfelt appreciation" to everyone involved.)

Once trust is in place, administrators can share leadership by encouraging and empowering everyone in the organization. As an example of what not to do, I once worked for a superintendent whose most enthusiastic response to any new idea or suggestion was, "It's harmless." Needless to say, people didn't feel very supported or empowered. Most quit trying to offer suggestions for improvement. It was a culture buster.

What works best is to practice what author George A. Goens calls "soft leadership for hard time" by concentrating on relationships, values, and individual freedom. It's a little like being part pastor, part parent, and part partner.

This means giving teachers and students permission and a safe haven for practicing and making mistakes. In his top-of-the-charts bestseller *Blink* (2007), Malcolm Gladwell calls it "being in command, and out of control"—providing overall guidance with few restrictive directives, while allowing people to function without explaining everything they do.

All this requires the leader to be proactive, visible, realistic, and willing to bend the rules ("creative insubordination") occasionally for the sake of the culture. It also helps if the principal or superintendent can become a "prospector" by researching, cultivating, soliciting, and negotiating new resources for the school. This is a surefire way to strengthen the culture and convert holdouts at the same time.

Do all this, and make it fun for everyone. Then, you will have essentially mastered the art of servant leadership and culture building.

Enough generalities. You want specific help. You want to know what to do and how to start. You want practical ideas you can try in your school starting tomorrow morning. Coming up.

Chapters 8 through 12 will offer more concrete ways to target and tailor the school culture to each of the separate groups of stakeholders—students, staff, parents, and community members. But first, below are a dozen action steps for improving your school climate that you can implement immediately. They have all worked for someone. Now it's your turn.

CULTURE-BUILDING ACTION STEPS

1. *Introduce your staff (and yourself) to the next generation of long-range planning called Appreciative Inquiry.* Where most traditional strategic planning models still focus on problems and solutions, Appreciative Inquiry is all about building on existing strengths. The underlying premise is that organizations (e.g., schools, communities, and businesses) move and grow toward whatever they routinely ask questions about.

The process assumes that the organization is already doing well and seeks information to move to the next level. It articulates possibilities and compels participants to inquire deeply into the culture and cocreate a preferred future (common vision).

Advocates believe schools and other organizations become the answers to the questions they ask themselves. More simply, the nature of the inquiry determines the nature of the outcomes. When the school relentlessly asks about what's working and how to make it even better, it multiplies its strengths and defines new potentials.

Appreciative Inquiry practitioners use lots of different data to find answers, determine direction, and make choices. But they rely most heavily on the stories that stakeholders tell about what they are most proud of within the culture, why it works, what feels good about it, and what they want to achieve next. The implication of the stories and the dreams of the storytellers, then, becomes the future of the organization. The common ground revealed by the stories becomes the basis for specific actionable goals.

The first step in Appreciative Inquiry planning in schools is for the key leaders to commit to creating opportunities for all interested stakeholders to participate in the visioning process.

Proponents claim this approach is the most productive way to "grow" the organizational culture because (a) it engages everyone in the organization; (b) it is inspiring and open-ended; (c) it is upbeat and builds positive momentum, which brings out the best in those involved and energizes the entire organization; and (d) it's fun.

If you're tired of dealing with negatives and want to boost your school's culture through proactive planning and action, Appreciative Inquiry may be just what you're looking for. If you want to learn more, check out *Appreciative Inquiry: A Positive Revolution in Change* by David Cooperrider and Diana Whitney (Berrett-Koehler Publishers, 2005).

2. *Work on creating and expanding connections (relationships).* Connections are the core of the culture, and relationships are the way leaders get things done.

It's the leader's job to foster collegiality and teamwork based on collaboration. After all, the most effective way to change the culture is to change people by changing the relationships.

> At the heart of learning is the leader's relationships with followers.
>
> —David Gergen, author of *Eyewitness to Power,* 2001

The key to building a healthy culture that works for everyone is developing strong internal and external connections in all directions. That includes students, staff, parents, school board members, unions, community organizations, social service agencies, politicians, philanthropists, businesses, the faith community, health care professionals, and anyone else who can help (or hurt) the school's future.

Most human resources specialists agree that the best ways to develop positive relationships with various audiences are to

- Be real (authentic).
- Show interest.
- Listen.
- Simplify.
- Bring renewed enthusiasm and humor to the table.
- Help out.
- Tell the truth.
- Be on time.
- Empathize.

As with all executives, your leadership is only as good as your relationships. That's why, when you're the leader of the school, the entire community should be your network. As with fine tea, relationships need time to steep and mellow. The best time to start steeping is now.

> A principal has to be a special leader. We have to help people recapture the meaning of the work and we have to talk about the things that touch their hearts.
>
> —Lee G. Bolman, University of Missouri at Kansas City

3. *Dare to discuss core values.* Talk about baseline principles and beliefs. Don't fumble or mumble. Speak out. Stand up for what the school stands for. It's not sissy, corny, or touchy-feely. It's leading. How else can you inspire exceptional performance?

Teachers and other staff members will show up and do the job for money. But they will perform miracles only if they are inspired.

4. *Use language to shape the culture.* Words are powerful. The right ones can make people feel good, try harder, and achieve more. If you want a culture that runs full throttle, be generous with authentic praise. Tell people (at all levels) when you like them, believe them, support them, trust them, respect them, and admire them.

But choose your words carefully. Avoid too many military or sports metaphors. Be careful what you call people and how you label staff members who are not classroom teachers. Some are sensitive about negative references such as "nonteaching" or "unlicensed." (I know a minister who makes it clear that he doesn't consider clerical personnel as part of the "professional staff." And they don't like it. What does that make them—"unprofessional?")

In some schools, the term "classified" is acceptable—but it's rather vague. If you come up with a better label or category, let the rest of us know about it.

5. *Spend 50 percent of your time with the middle 70 percent of your staff.* Some leaders devote an inordinate amount of time working with the bottom 15 percent of the staff, trying to fix the unfixable. Others choose to invest most of their effort in the top 15 percent, because it's easier and more fun.

But the most effective school leaders spend most of their time with the largest (and most often neglected) segment of their staff—the middle 70 percent. This group is the heart of the organization. Recognize them. Work with them. The culture isn't going anywhere without them.

6. *Use the power of good news.* Everyone talks about the problems and failings of public education. So be sure that someone talks about all the good stuff that happens in schools as well. Bad news is contagious. And it depresses the culture. Good news is equally infectious, but it elevates the culture.

Some leaders begin or end every meeting with a round-up of good news. There always is some. I also know school districts that hold annual Caring Youth Recognition events to spread the good news about the positive contributions kids make to the community.

At one such event, I heard a father give an award to two teenagers who had spent *every Saturday for four years* coming to his house to befriend his autistic son, who has underdeveloped social skills. The two students never missed a Saturday, summer or winter, and they walked when they couldn't get a ride. Without them, the son would have been pretty much isolated and friendless.

To top off the presentation, the father called his son out of the audience to help give out the awards. The son not only handed out the certificates to the two teens but also gave each recipient a giant bear hug that lifted them off the floor. It was a moving moment for everyone in the room.

That one story of good news did more to inspire and uplift the young people, teachers, administrators, and parents present than a boxcar load of positive test results could ever do.

Good news is always an elixir for the organization. Don't hoard it or be stingy with it. No culture ever overdosed on good news.

7. *Make some physical changes in the environment.* Consider substituting round tables for the old-fashioned, traditional long conference tables, and even for some student desks. Sometimes, when you change the physical configuration, you alter the culture as well.

Have you heard about the Cold War summit meetings where U.S. and Soviet officials could not even agree on who should sit at the head (or foot) of the conference table? The dispute threatened to scuttle the proceedings before they actually began. The solution? A round table. Everyone is equal at a round table.

Some private schools have had success by replacing the customary student and teacher desks with round tables. They claim the following benefits:

- Everyone is "invited to the table."
- There is no front row or back row.
- Everyone is engaged—there is no place to hide.
- Students listen more and tend to be better prepared.

Why wouldn't this approach work in a public school as well?

On another level, I used to work for a superintendent who insisted that the school board replace the traditional "airplane" wing table with a round one, so that board members were forced to face each other. Some (including me for a while) thought it was a weird idea.

But his rationale was that the purpose of board meetings was for members to interact with each other and practice joint decision making—not just to hold audiences with their "peasants and petitioners."

And when boards and other panels sit side by side at a long table, they tend to play to the audience, either those present in the meeting room or those watching at home via TV, rather than to each other. In fact, they often can't even see each other. As it turned out, the round table was a hit at board meetings. And I was converted. A round table worked for King Arthur. It just might work in your school, too,

8. *While you're at it, try having fewer desks and offices than you have administrators or assistants.* It's one way to force administrative personnel to share and to be out and about more of the time. It almost mandates Management While Walking Around (MWWA). Wouldn't that be good for your school culture? It works for executives at the Honda Corporation. What do the Japanese know that we don't?

9. *Dare to be silly to model or support core values.* We all know examples of administrators agreeing to all kinds of embarrassments (e.g., being doused in a dunk tank) to achieve goals consistent with the school's culture, such as reading a certain number of books or raising a predetermined amount of money for charity.

When Bob Tift, president of Benilde–St. Margaret's High School, allowed students to shave his beard after they brought in a record number of contributions to the local food shelves, the school was flooded with humorous computer graphic portrayals of what Tift might look like without his signature beard. (Even his wife and children had never seen him without a beard.) It was fun for everyone for a good cause. It was a culture builder. There's nothing silly about that.

10. *Use a secret weapon to give your school culture an edge.* Believe it or not, preparation is the forgotten secret weapon of school leadership. Remember the Boy Scout motto, "Be prepared"? No matter what you think of the organization, you have to admire the motto.

Unfortunately, some school officials forget how critical preparation is to continued peak performance. Skimping on preparation is really preparing to fail and to take your culture down with you.

> *We are all . . . saving ourselves for the Senior Prom. But many of us forget that somewhere along the way we have to learn to dance.*
>
> —Alan Harrington
> writer

Most of us know some principals or superintendents who think they're good enough, smart enough, and experienced enough that they don't need to spend much time preparing. They're missing the point. Even champions need practice and preparation.

The best in the business are always prepared. One of the best-kept secrets of successful culture building is that it takes a lot of preparation to appear spontaneous. You never outgrow the need to prepare.

Most public school administrators are well trained and hardworking. So why do some create stronger cultures than others? You guessed it. The prize usually goes to the one who is best prepared.

Preparation provides you and your culture an advantage. If you are not preparing every day, you're shortchanging your staff, students, parents, and community members—the entire culture and yourself.

It's no coincidence that baseball's Hall of Famers Joe DiMaggio and Ted Williams took more batting practice than all their teammates combined. They wanted to be better prepared than anyone else on the field. They knew that's the only way to get to the top. And stay there. The Boy Scouts had it right all along.

When you are unprepared or underprepared, you are much more likely to make false starts, wrong turns, or questionable choices that undermine the culture of the organization.

No matter how seasoned or experienced you are, you still need to prepare every day for

- Holding conferences
- Giving pep talks
- Handling confrontations

- Responding to questions
- Explaining
- Selling ideas
- Dealing with crises

. . . and much more.

But how do you prepare for the unknown and the uncertain? It may be easier than you think. The following preparation strategies have worked for many of your peers:

- Do your homework.
- Conduct "walk-throughs."
- Ask "what if" questions.
- Brainstorm alternative scenarios.
- Practice visualization.
- Rehearse.

The point is to do whatever it takes to anticipate possibilities, weigh choices, and practice a variety of responses. That's why former New York City mayor Rudolph Giuliani urges leaders to instill a "culture of preparation" throughout the organization. Good leaders pass on the preparation ethic to everyone else in the culture.

According to Giuliani, successful leaders prepare relentlessly. "Preparation is the key to success. . . . Leaders can possess brilliance, extraordinary vision, fate, even luck—but no one can perform without preparation," he says.

Could the Boy Scouts and Rudy Giuliani both be wrong? Don't bet on it. Motivational speaker and writer Harvey Mackay tells the story of a New England farmer who could "sleep while the wind blows." While other farmers scurried and scrambled around when storm warnings came late at night, he slept soundly, because all the necessary preparations (e.g., barn doors bolted, hay covered, and so on) had already been made. Like the New England farmer, if you prepare for contingencies, you do your culture a favor. And you can sleep while the wind blows.

11. *Hire culture builders.* How you hire and whom you hire says a lot about you and the culture of the organization.

Each new hire alters the mix and changes the culture to some degree. If you make a mistake, it may be a mistake the organization has to live with for 20 years or more. That's why it always pays to keep the culture in mind when recruiting and hiring new personnel—

First-rate people hire first-rate people, second-rate people hire third-rate people.

—Lee Rosten
writer

for any position. Hire people who will strengthen the culture and help move the organization closer to its true mission.

Remember that who you are is who you tend to attract; so be wary of just hiring people you feel most comfortable with. For the sake of the culture, you want to hire people who are better than you are.

Hire for diversity. Don't be afraid to bring a maverick onboard. You need new employees who will upgrade your team, not just carbon copies or cookie-cutter clones of what you already have. If a prospect doesn't feel right, back off. This is one area where it's okay to trust your gut.

12. *Get out more often.* Nationwide research involving executives from all fields shows that leaders get more new ideas from conferences and seminars than from any other single source. Likewise, they get more inspiration from conferences than from networks, peers, journals, or online resources. (Incidentally, "the boss" ranked near the bottom as a source of both new ideas and inspiration.)

The meaning is clear. To get new ideas and renewed excitement to bring to your culture, you need to go outside of the culture occasionally. Don't spend all your time talking to the same people. Cultures, like all organic entities, often grow stronger through cross-pollination.

The value of the dozen strategies above isn't that they are panaceas or quick-fix solutions, but that they are catalysts that can trigger additional ideas, which may be even more effective. The point is that anything you can do to serve the needs of all those connected to the school, the better leader you are. Remember Amos the prophet?

The legendary former CEO of General Electric, Jack Welch, likens workplace obstacles to a house. There are horizontal barriers (internal walls), such as compartmentalization; vertical barriers (floors and ceilings), such as a bureaucratic hierarchy; and external barriers (external walls), such as practices that keep parents at a distance. It's your job to tear down the walls, remove the obstacles, and open up the culture for everyone.

Of course, in school, the culture begins and ends with kids. Without them, there is no culture and no need for a culture. That's why Chapter 8 focuses on user-friendly ways to ensure that the unique culture of your school works for all students.

8

Don't Teach the Canaries Not to Sing

Creating a School Culture That Works for All Students

Student learning cannot occur without mindful attention to school culture and climate.

> —Jeffrey Glanz, educator and author of
> *What Every Principal Should Know*
> *About Cultural Leadership* (2006)

All students are created equal. They are endowed by their creator with an inalienable right to an education that will accord them life, liberty, and the pursuit of happiness.

> —A slight alteration of the Declaration of
> Independence created by educational
> researcher Gerald W. Bracay

———————————— ✀ ————————————

It's no secret that the "canaries" in the title of this book represent students in our schools. The premise of the metaphor is that as educators, we sometimes—knowingly or unwittingly—stifle the voices and silence the songs of some of the canaries entrusted to our care.

There's also another reason why canaries are an apt symbol for students. In the old days, it was common practice for mining companies to introduce canaries into their deepest and most hazardous mine shafts. The frailty and fragility of the canaries made them well suited as an early warning system. If the underground air became poisonous or dangerously polluted, the canaries were affected much quicker than the miners themselves. When the canaries began to drop and die, the miners knew they were in trouble.

It's the same in schools. When the canaries become still and drop out, it's a sign of an unhealthy climate. Unfortunately, it happens somewhere— or a lot of somewheres—every day. Some of our most vulnerable students aren't making it. There is something stagnant, foul, or polluted in some school environments that is harmful for certain students. That's either unacceptable or intolerable—whichever is worse.

Every canary is precious. This means that the culture of the school must be all-inclusive. That's why we call them "public" schools.

Children may be 20 percent of the population, but they are 100 percent of the future.

—Frank B. Tyack
Stanford University

The school culture needs to work for all kids, or it's not working at all. It's not good enough for the culture to accommodate the needs of just the White, bright, and polite kids— or just the sweet-smelling, well-scrubbed, well-dressed, and well-behaved kids—or just the kids whose parents speak fluent English, have jobs and investment portfolios, and come to PTA meetings.

The culture has to serve all children—including the tattooed, the spiked, and the pierced. In a healthy culture, the teachers love even the kids who throw up on them. In discussing his work as a marketing specialist in Minneapolis, Ken Greer says, "We are searching to find the fresh starters, the upstarts, the restarts, and the start-ups in the world." He could just as well have been talking about a fully functioning school culture.

The school culture has to be accepting and available even to the dropout who may someday decide to drop back in. This is what happened to the recipient of a Distinguished Alumni award at a recognized Catholic high school. As a successful senior, majoring in Spanish and hoping to become a teacher, the student (name withheld) became discouraged and depressed, dropped out, and went to work as a waitress.

One day, her former English teacher came into the restaurant where she worked. The girl tried to avoid her former mentor, but the teacher spied her and asked, "What are you doing here?" The girl reluctantly recounted her story. The teacher then took her hands, looked her in the eyes, and said, "My dear, you will make a wonderful teacher. You must pursue your dream."

The girl heeded the advice, returned to school, and graduated. Later, she completed college, became a teacher, and helped found a new Spanish immersion school. That's why she was singled out as a distinguished alumna.

That's the way it is with good schools. They never give up on any student. At least, that's how it is supposed to work.

But how well are our schools really doing in working for all students? "Not good enough" is an understatement. Too many kids drop out or fail. Too many others lose their zest for learning, their curiosity, their confidence, and their hope for the future. A few even develop scholionophobia—an overwhelming fear of school. Too many canaries stop singing. In a small way, my son was an example.

Like many children, when my son was seven years old, he loved to draw and color. He often spent hours in his room entertaining himself with paper and crayons.

Fortunately, his teachers encouraged his interest at school by allowing him (and others) to draw whatever they wanted, however they wanted to draw it. Then we moved to a different city.

On one of the first few days in a new school, the teacher's art lesson consisted of passing out crayons and pages ripped from a coloring book. This was a new experience for my son, but he cheerfully colored away without much regard for staying within the lines. That had never been part of the bargain before.

When the "lesson" was over, the teacher held up my son's work for ridicule saying, "This is the worst coloring I've ever seen."

Needless to say, my son came home mortified, crushed, and stifled. His mother tried to console him by saying that she still thought his coloring was best; but this teacher had a different standard. It didn't help much.

My wife then called the teacher and "unloaded." It got the teacher's attention. The next day, the art lesson was repeated. This time, my son dutifully and painstakingly stayed within the lines. At lesson's end, the teacher again held up his work, this time lavishing praise and proclaiming, "This is the best coloring in the class." It was a transparent gesture that even a seven-year-old could see through.

The damage was done. My son never drew or colored on his own for fun again. The world probably wasn't deprived of a great artistic talent. But a little boy lost an outlet and a form of creative expression that he loved.

I know the teacher involved. She wasn't a bad teacher or a mean, unfeeling person. She was just thoughtless, clueless, and misguided. And she taught one more canary not to sing.

Perhaps teaching one small boy to give up drawing is no monumental deal. But teaching thousands of teenage girls to dislike or distance themselves from science subjects is a *huge* deal. So is teaching legions of boys that being smart isn't "cool" and that studying isn't macho.

It's an even bigger deal to teach large numbers of students—of both sexes—to be afraid of failing or afraid of even trying. Even worse is teaching some kids that the school won't help them and doesn't have a place for them anymore.

Yet, all this bad stuff and more happens in our schools. Some of it is happening in your school. The culture isn't working for all kids. We can do better. We should do better. Just maybe, we have to do better.

Of course, no school culture can be so good that every child succeeds. But all school cultures can be good enough so that every child has a chance to succeed. We're not there yet.

Naturally, there are some negative, insensitive, or damaging school practices that we should eliminate; but just fixing what's broken isn't sufficient. (Remember Chapter 7?) An all-inclusive school culture can't be realized by remedies alone.

Neither can it be achieved by overarching, sweeping reforms or lofty pronouncements. A fully functioning culture results only from the accumulation of layer upon layer of small acts and adjustments. To benefit all students, what most school cultures need today is an old-fashioned makeover.

We can't become what we need to be by remaining what we are.

—Oprah Winfrey
legendary TV
talk show host

It is no secret that Americans suffer from makeover mania. We're obsessed with updating, upgrading, reinventing, and improving everything from our houses to our hairdos. Actually, it's not a bad fixation.

Almost everyone and everything can benefit from periodic polishing, burnishing, and modernizing in order to remain fresh, relevant, and interesting. School cultures are no exception. Even the best schools with the best cultures can get better.

This is a lesson that leading principals and superintendents strive to get across to all staff members. Better yet, they take it to heart themselves. If you are up to giving your school environment a makeover, to make it better for all students, it can be easier than you think.

As it turns out, most makeovers do not entail completely scrapping the old and replacing it with something new and different. Instead, makeovers usually involve reinforcing what already exists and making it even better. It is mostly a matter of building on current strengths, sharpening existing principles and practices, and adding some new ones.

A makeover tends to be more like a tune-up than a complete engine replacement. Even modest modifications and improvements can add up to a significant makeover and transform your culture from good to great. It's worth the effort.

If you want examples, following is a sampling of 30 reality-tested ways to create a more student-friendly culture in your school. If you're in a hurry, you can make it your own personal, one-month makeover plan.

30 Ways in 30 Days to a Better School Environment

Day 1. Recommit to high standards. All students benefit from being stretched. Anything less is a cop-out. If you think standards haven't slipped a bit, here are just three sample questions from the eighth-grade final exam for Salina, Kansas, in 1895:

1. A wagon bed is 2 ft. deep, 10 ft. long and 3 ft. wide. How many bushels of wheat will it hold?

2. Give 2 rules for spelling words with a final "e." Name two exceptions under each rule.

3. Name all the republics of Europe and give the capital of each.

Busywork is an insult.

—Frank McCourt
author of *Teacher Man* (2006)

Admittedly, not all students reached the eighth grade back then; but it still gives a whole new meaning to "only an eighth-grade education."

Raising the bar can help everyone.

Day 2. Let students develop new rituals and ceremonies to honor the values of the culture.

As part of opening a new high school, I once worked with a group of students who had to develop the school's traditions, symbols, mascot, school song, and rituals from scratch. They were uncomfortable and resistant for a while. At first, they just wanted to copy the traditions from their old school. But eventually, they broke new ground, created a culture of their own, and, in the process, built a powerful tie and lasting loyalty to the school. The more students invest in the school's culture, the more commitment they have to preserving and protecting it.

In 34 years as an educator, I have never seen academic rigor not work.

—Pat Harvey, superintendent

Day 3. Require counselors to call the parents of at-risk students every Friday—with good news. Many parents have never received that kind of call from the school.

Day 4. Arrange for a real driving-under-the-influence (DUI) trial to be held at school for students to observe firsthand. That's about as riveting experiential learning as you can find.

(Continued)

(Continued)

Day 5. Adopt a "no immunization, no entry" rule for kindergartners. It's another way to put the "healthy" into a healthy environment.

Day 6. Initiate an International Baccalaureate program at the elementary school level. Include world language instruction and an optional foreign language immersion school for interested families. I know one school system that is even introducing a preschool International Baccalaureate program.

Day 7. Pay attention to transitions. This is where we lose many students. I remember as a teenager changing to a new school, where I was given a map and a class schedule and left on my own. I got lost the first day. In many ways, I remained lost for an entire year. You don't want that to happen to any of your students.

Ninth graders seem especially vulnerable. That's why many schools, including Highland Park High School in Topeka, Kansas, have developed Freshman Academies, schools-within-a-school, or special bridge-building programs designed to change the culture of the ninth-grade year.

These programs typically include off-site "respect" retreats, team-building exercises, on-site mentoring, reduced class size, classes on social competencies, and immediate referral at the first sign a student is starting to slip. Some schools have also had success with a monthly Breakfast Club, where freshmen are matched with seniors who serve as academic and social mentors.

Seamless transitions are a sign of a healthy school culture. How well are your students making the leap from one level to another?

Day 8. Introduce a little quiet time into the school schedule. A little quietude allows students and adults to regroup, "recoup," and center themselves to continue the hectic pace of learning.

It works in the Cambridge, Massachusetts, Friends School, where every Tuesday all students (preK to eighth grade) sit silently in a circle for 30 minutes. No whispering is allowed, but the youngest children are allowed to color or draw. The school believes in the value of uninterrupted quiet time to promote creative thinking, problem solving, and self-reliance.

Couldn't you use a little more quiet time? Couldn't everyone else in the school as well?

Day 9. Pay special attention to immigrants and refugees. Train your teachers to help ease the adjustment of newcomers to our society.

In her classic work, *The Middle of Everywhere* (2003), Mary Pipher describes the kind of school culture that works for little children coping with a strange new world: "The most important cultural brokers are school teachers. Schools are the first line institutions in acculturation where children receive solid information about their new world. Almost all refugee families have a tremendous respect for education and educators. And our schools do not let them down. I have met many heroic teachers who, among other responsibilities, become the antidotes to media and ads."

Pipher was talking about the Lincoln, Nebraska, schools. But her remarks fit all schools today. Pipher has it right. If our schools fail with our exploding immigrant population, we're failing a good part of our nation's future.

There are schools that create what civil rights activist Jesse Jackson calls the "illusion of inclusion," and other schools that actually do include everyone. See that your school falls into the second category, and make Jesse proud.

Day 10. Beef up support for minority groups in your school—especially Black male students. If we can't or don't close the achievement gap between minority and majority students, we're contributing to a polarized society.

I know a school that sponsors a "Boys to Men" program designed to help African American boys change the stereotype, improve grades and attendance, and handle social situations responsibly. The group meets several times a month, using a "restorative justice circle" style to talk about problems, go over real-life situations faced by the students, and address issues of underachievement. The group also balances talk with action by participating in civil rights tours, completing service-learning projects, and mentoring younger minority students.

Some other communities have launched "Right Turn Projects" to help young African American men by providing role models, conducting literacy training, finding jobs, helping students earn a high school diploma, walking participants through the social service system, and helping clear up criminal records.

Of course, Black males are not the only minority group in schools that need special support. Some high schools initiated a dropout prevention program for Hispanic students such as ALMAS, which stands for Anglos Latinos Motivados A Superarse (Latin Americans Motivated to Succeed). One of the group's successes has been the creation of a popular antismoking song. Other schools have formed special support groups or programs for different minorities, including gay and lesbian students.

The point is that there is no one way to support and boost the achievement of minority students. The important thing is to find the way that meets the needs in your school. Minority students are canaries too. Don't let your school teach them not to sing.

Day 11. Teach your teachers (and parents) that there are multiple intelligences, including word smarts, number smarts, picture smarts, music smarts, body smarts, people smarts, self smarts, emotional smarts, and street smarts. When everyone believes that every child is "smart about something," you will have achieved an accepting and empowering school culture.

(Continued)

(Continued)

Day 12. Encourage our teachers to make science entertaining. Have you heard about a group of teachers who put on an annual "Physics Circus" to prove that physics is fun? One of their demonstrations involves dropping one of them from a height of 20 feet while shooting a ball at him to show the interaction of gravity and projectiles. I've also read about another teacher who uses theme park rides to teach the laws of physics. This is the kind of stuff that makes teaching meaningful, builds lasting student memories, and creates a dynamic culture.

If you can't hire these guys, help your own teachers to introduce some fun and excitement into the science curriculum.

Day 13. Introduce your students to MATHCOUNTS, a nonprofit program to promote middle school math achievement. Its goal is to recognize math prowess on a par with the current recognition of athletic prowess. The organization holds a nationwide competition and maintains a Web site featuring a "Problem of the Week" and other math challenges.

Day 14. Help organize a juvenile diversion program in your community. The purpose is to provide a positive alternative to formal court proceedings for motivated male and female first-time juvenile offenders. Where it works best, the program is operated by a community board that meets at least six times a year to hear petitions and evidence and determine alternative consequences.

Day 15. Start a "Socrates Café" evening event in your school. The activity, which has spread to many communities throughout the country, features open-ended discussions (idea and opinion exchange) on a selected philosophical, ethical, or controversial issue. Usually, participants nominate several possible questions for the evening, and then vote to select the night's topic. No resolution of the issue is expected; and the only ground rule is, "Attack an idea, but not a person." Who says American schools don't teach kids how to think?

Day 16. Initiate an all-day kindergarten option if you don't already have one. It may not be for every pupil; but it is a logical extension for those children accustomed to full-day preschool or daycare programs.

Day 17. Allow the school's student newspaper to operate independently of the school administration. It's a little risky, but it demonstrates confidence in the student newspaper staff and faculty advisor. More important, it breeds responsibility. That's what we are supposed to be teaching, isn't it?

Day 18. Promote a weeklong, voluntary Habitat for Humanity experience for students as a substitute for the traditional "spring break" revelry.

Day 19. Let students make some of the school rules. But be prepared for some surprises and unexpected twists. For example, at the new Minneapolis Public Library, young people drafted the ground rules for the teen center, including, "No adults can hang in the center without a teen chaperone."

Letting students in on the rule making makes them coauthors of the culture. The students are stronger for the experience—and so is the culture.

Day 20. Start an All-Boys Book Club in your school. It will work best if led by a popular male instructor. This is another way to chip away at the growing gender academic achievement gap.

Day 21. Organize a student-run "credit union." Recruit a good economics teacher as advisor. It's a great way for kids to learn about money management, interest rates, credit, monitoring accounts, and balancing checkbooks, and it helps students gain confidence and save money at the same time.

Day 22. Initiate a mentoring program for young student writers. One way to start is to pair the student writers with graduate students who are in a Master of Fine Arts in Creative Writing program. The grad students work with individuals and small groups on writing, reading, editing, revising, and experimenting with different writing styles. A good way to culminate and celebrate the experience each year is to sponsor public reading of works by both mentors and young writers.

Day 23. Get students excited about energy savings. Some schools sponsor a Students for Energy Efficiency (SEE) program that recruits students to check the school daily, looking for energy wasters. Besides promoting prudent energy use, it is also a good way to give students a sense of purpose, build pride in the school, and teach social responsibility all at the same time.

Day 24. Promote fitness and wellness as part of a healthy school environment. Surpass new government standards on healthy lunch choices. I know of one high school that hired a professional chef to create better tastier, healthier, and more attractive meals. The district also maintains a café open to the public and sells take-home meals to staff and the public. Another district in the Midwest has gone a step further by allowing the kids to vote on the "coolest new veggie" to add to the school lunch menu.

In addition to more nutritious lunches, stock vending machines with fruit and healthy snacks. And charge noticeably more for candy and soda—if you sell these items at all.

Other healthy initiatives can include converting part of the gym space to a fitness center open to the public and developing a walking path around the school grounds for use by students, staff, and community members.

(Continued)

(Continued)

Day 25. Adopt a "Trading Spaces" theme. Have boys paint (decorate) the girls' bathroom and vice versa. It's probably wise to have the boys work with a female artist and the girls work with a male artist to develop designs for preapproval. If you're lucky, Home Depot or another retailer will sponsor the project and provide the supplies free of charge.

This is a good way to spruce up the school, boost school spirit, build relationships, and have fun all at once. Some schools go even further and allow seniors to decorate one hallway with a mural depicting class highlights or the class legacy to the school. Creating symbols to illustrate the culture is a powerful way to reinforce and pass it on.

Day 26. Create more opportunities for fun during the school day. A school without fun denies the nature of childhood. Everyone works and learns better when there is fun to be had. That's why Harvard University once hired a "Fun Czar" to build school spirit and help stressed-out students unwind.

You may not want to go that far, but you can organize some games and silly activities during state testing periods or final exams to lighten the mood, relieve tension, and foster relationships.

Day 27. Dare to add a motorcycle curriculum. Think the biker set is unreachable? Try having your Industrial Tech class design, build, and customize a chopper (motorcycle). It works at Kennedy High School in Bloomington, Minnesota, where the finished bike each term is sold, with the proceeds going back into the program.

Supporters claim the project fuels student interest, sparks creativity, and teaches a variety of skills, including networking. Besides, all the students are in "hog heaven." How's that for a culture builder?

Day 28. Try to improve student achievement by changing how the classroom looks. A growing number of elementary schools across the country are updating classroom décor by adding recessed lighting, comfy chairs and sofas, area rugs, wooden tables, and occasional classic music. It makes the classroom feel more like someone's room in a house.

The trend is based on brain research showing that a sterile (institutional-looking) classroom limits learning, while a more relaxed, homelike atmosphere helps students focus and learn more.

Day 29. Start a "Check and Connect" dropout prevention program. In this approach, developed by the Bush Foundation (no relation to the presidents with the same name), "check and connect monitors" strive to build a special personal connection and relationship with individual at-risk students. The goal is to improve attendance and engagement in school and to keep each student in school until graduation.

The monitors make a long-term commitment to their protégés, check regularly on progress (or lack of it), and help the students develop key survival skills. Typically, each monitor is assigned 50 students per year. Cost of the program is about $1,400 per pupil. Too expensive? It's a bargain compared to the cost of dropping out.

Day 30. Review efforts to improve adolescent literacy. It's never too late to help teenagers become successful readers. Despite the challenges of teenage angst, anger, and apathy, there are programs that work.

For example, the Strategic Instruction Model (SIM) developed at the University of Kansas uses an array of supports for improving literacy in teens, including:

- Teaching students to create mental pictures of what they read
- Helping students to use paraphrasing to identify main points
- Developing memory techniques to aid students in vocabulary building
- Guiding students through developmental stages of writing (e.g., sentences, paragraphs, entire essays)

As school leader, it's your job to keep your teachers looking until they find the strategies that work best with your kids. A good school doesn't back up, back off, or back down. It doesn't settle, turn away, or give up. It's part of their culture. Is it part of yours?

By now, you're probably thinking: "Nice list. But easier said than done." Of course, you can't make over your school's culture in 30 days. But if you do something—even just one small act—each day to make your school culture better, you can achieve phenomenal results quicker than you think. Yes, I said "phenomenal results." And that's not an overstatement.

Remember that the list above is only representative. If you don't like any of these ideas, there is an infinity of other possibilities. There is no end of measures that can improve the quality of your school's climate, such as:

- Bring in panels of top-flight scientists to share their exciting work and spur student interest in science.
- Offer signing (sign language) as part of the second-language curriculum (especially where deaf students are present in the student population).
- Build on Search Institute's 40 Developmental Assets for Kids (e.g., sense of purpose, cultural competence, and a positive view of the future) by highlighting "An Asset a Week" throughout the school and the community.

- Ban fragrances that pose allergic health risks for some students.
- Recruit volunteers to provide afterschool tutoring in low-income housing complexes.
- Encourage coaches to stress character education as part of the athletic experience.

Well, you get the idea. The list could go on and on. The point is to keep trying to make your school environment work better for all students. Anything that makes the culture more inclusive, increases the odds for student success, humanizes the institution, or creates more second chances counts.

Business and homemaking maven Martha Stewart naturally has a list of success tips for entrepreneurs. The one I like best is, "Make it beautiful." If every adult in your school does something every day to make the school experience more beautiful, you can create a better school than you ever imagined possible.

Of course, some people fear the cost of doing what it takes to keep all the canaries singing. Education is expensive. Good education is even more expensive, but it's not as costly as moviemaking or professional sports— or war. Another difference is that it's worth it!

The good news, however, is that many of the actions needed to make the school culture work for all kids cost little or nothing. They just take the will to act and the energy to try. I have a T-shirt that says, "We don't want your money, just a little change." That wouldn't be a bad slogan for creating a better climate in your school.

Now, I'll end this chapter with a little common horse sense. Business columnist Tim McGuire suggests that people are a lot like horses, and what works in training horses can work in motivating people as well. In training horses, when the horse is not doing what you want, it is often because he doesn't understand what you want. If instruction does not make sense, the horse will resist it. Good trainers learn to work with the horse rather than trying to force him to do things that don't make sense.

As it turns out, all that horses seem to want is "happiness, joy, understanding, fun, and peaceful interaction." Whoa! Kids want the same things. If the school culture provides these elements, students will respond positively. It only makes perfect horse sense.

Enough with the animal metaphors (canaries and horses) already! Let's talk kids. The bottom line is that you run the school. The school is for kids. Whatever helps kids is good. Whatever hurts kids is bad. Do good. Dump the bad. It's that simple.

But what ultimately determines whether the school succeeds or fails is not the principal, superintendent, or school board but the teachers and other staff members. They make the good things (or bad things) happen. And they're part of the culture too. If the culture doesn't work well for them, it won't work for students either. Which brings us to Chapter 9.

9

Use All the Gifts (Assets)

Creating a School Culture That Works for Staff

A positive learning culture cannot be nurtured without teacher involvement, nor can there be a positive climate without satisfied teachers.

—Jeffrey Glanz, educator and author
of *What Every Principal Should Know
About Cultural Leadership* (2006)

————————— ✦ —————————

There are many ways to build a culture that benefits those who work in it. Google, the Internet search engine behemoth, does it by providing pace-setting perks, including free, chef-prepared meals, on-site day care, medical treatment, dry cleaning, laundry services, and workout facilities, as well as 12 weeks of maternity leave at 75 percent full pay and permission to spend up to 20 percent of the work day pursuing individual projects and ideas. Sound good?

Don't get excited. Those kinds of perks are not going to happen anytime soon in your school or any other public school in America. That's okay because they are not necessary to a successful culture.

In order for the school culture to work for all staff members, it doesn't have to make the job easier, more comfortable, more "cushy," or more glamorous. It only has to make the job possible, more rewarding, and more fun. It starts with how you think about your staff, including teachers, aides, clerks, cooks, custodians, and bus drivers

Some principals, superintendents, pretenders, look-alikes, and wannabe school leaders view their staff members as lackeys or lesser beings. Of course, this pretty much precludes them from ever getting admitted to the Administrators Hall of Fame.

The truth is that school employees are not property, serfs, automatons, pawns, or chattel. Instead, they are the organization's (and your) greatest assets. If you don't believe this, you are putting yourself and your school at a disadvantage.

Every person on your staff is a one-of-a-kind intellectual asset. And each possesses some special gift or gifts that can make your school better. The trick is to tap into all the assets at your disposal.

There! The secret is out. The key to creating a culture that works for all the staff is to start with the assets. There are always more assets than you think, and you should focus on the gifts, not on the deficiencies. Successful culture building, then, is mostly a matter of asset development (making the most of each and every asset and using all the gifts).

When you think of your staff members as unique assets (a treasure trove of energy and new ideas), it changes everything. You just naturally care for them as if they were precious jewels—which, in fact, they are. This means protecting and polishing each individual and placing them in a setting that shows off their best qualities and inner beauty.

This may be your most important role as school leader. If you fail to unleash the talents of your teachers, you've botched the job of culture building. After all, teachers can only be as good as the culture allows them to be.

The take-home lesson is that how you see the people who work for you becomes how they see themselves on the job; and how you treat them becomes a self-fulfilling prophecy. So how should you treat teachers and other team members?

Remember "servant leadership"? Remember "removing obstacles"? That's how.

One aspect of being a servant leader is being willing to do some of the heavy lifting and the dirty work. For example, I've known successful principals who actually get their own coffee, run their own copies, and answer their own phones, while their administrative assistants or secretaries work on something more important. I've known principals who cover for teachers on bus or cafeteria duty, and sometimes substitute in the classroom. I've even known a superintendent of a large urban school district who passed out programs at a high school music concert.

In her inspiring book *Our School* (2005), Joanne Jacobs tells the story of the principal of the Downtown Prep School in San José, California, who found himself cleaning excrement off a school wall. At first, the principal began to question why he was doing such dirty work; then he realized that it's all part of the job. "I have to deal with the crap they hand out," he said. Don't we all! That's part of being a servant leader. It's also part of building a school culture that works for all staff members.

Consequently, if you want to have maximum impact on the everyday environment in your school, you have to pitch in, help out, and treat your staff "right." What exactly does that mean?

It means treating teachers and others on the school staff as adults, as professionals, as friends, as partners, and as you want to be treated. It's that pesky Golden Rule again. It's been around for more than 2,000 years and it's still working. You just have to try it.

> You add value to people when you value them.
>
> —John C. Maxwell
> business writer

Likewise, it means treating all employees with respect and dignity. It also means treating all staff members fairly, which isn't necessarily the same as treating them equally or all the same, treating them as "insiders," and treating them as if they are capable of remarkable achievement.

It means getting to know staff members, at all levels, as real people with real lives outside of school. It means learning their "hot buttons" and what makes them tick and then giving them what they need to stay motivated and do their best work. Finally, it means that if you want to change people on your staff, you have to change the way you treat them.

> . . . Treat them greatly and they will show themselves to be great.
>
> —Ralph Waldo Emerson
> transcendental writer and
> philosopher

There are lots of ways to build a culture that benefits those who work in it. One of the best ways is simply to understand that all staff members are human beings and treat them accordingly. (Eat your heart out, Google!)

In my experience, there are at least six key core values or building blocks for constructing a school structure that treats all personnel right, capitalizes on all the assets, uses all the gifts, and maximizes peak performance by all those involved. I'm sure there are others. You may be able to add some of your own; but if you cover these six bases, you will be well on your way to a winning culture that brings out the best in everyone on the payroll.

1. FREEDOM

The best leadership advice I ever received was simply to point people in the right direction and get out of their way. Sometimes, a little discretion or elbow room is the greatest gift a servant leader can pass on to everyone in the organization. Allow the people who work for you enough latitude to do their jobs their way, and stand back. More often than not, they will

—————— ✂ ——————

Employees value a lot of things; money, power, and a title. But I find they most value freedom— primarily the freedom to fail.

—Steve Sabol
NFL filmmaker

surpass expectations, impress their friends, amaze their enemies, and make you look good. Skeptical? Dare to find out. You'll be glad you did.

Freedom ranks even ahead of low-cost heath insurance in what most teachers and other school personnel want from their jobs.

In the most productive cultures, employees— at all levels—are free to be original, try new things, and make mistakes.

I'm pretty sure you would like to work in an organization like that. So would every single person working for you. What's holding you back? Good school leaders have to be "freedom fighters"—willing to do battle to free up their staff to beat the odds and set new records.

—————— ✂ ——————

We tell them [employees] that there's a hole in their mistake bag and the mistakes all fall through.

—Karen Oman, award-winning small-business owner

Most star performers are looking for the three C's: a chance, a change, and a choice. As leader of the school, you are in a position to give your stars the freedom to have all three— a chance to show off what they can do; a change from deadly, repetitive routine and even deadlier predictability; and a choice of how to do their work as long as they achieve desired results (or better).

Freedom uncorks the bottle on creativity. If you give your teachers and support personnel the freedom to do and be their best, they will give you back a school culture that is the envy of the local principals' association.

2. EMPOWERMENT

There is probably no more overworked or tired term in the educators' lexicon than "empowerment." What can I say? It's still an absolutely essential component of a school culture that works for the staff. As long as teachers and other school employees are powerless, the assets are frozen and the gifts are locked away.

Of course, it takes a brave leader to relinquish power; but who would want to be any other kind of leader?

Some principals and superintendents are reluctant to give away any authority, because they fear losing power. They're missing the point. Empowerment actually multiplies the leader's power. What self-respecting principal or superintendent wouldn't be in favor of that?

Credible empowerment involves seeing in others what they don't see in themselves, opening doors to new opportunities, and giving away real control, not just phony or phantom authority.

Some of the quickest ways to energize your school culture through empowerment are to allow teachers and other staff members to voice opinions and disagree with decisions, to grant them discretionary control over part of the budget, and to give them power to make choices, make decisions, and make public statements about their work without prior review or approval.

An easy way to start is to allow employees to set some of their own targets, instead of imposing all their goals from above. My first experience with this form of empowerment was working with a performance appraisal system that allowed individuals to set some "personal goals," along with the traditional improvement steps suggested by their supervisor. The idea was to encourage people to target ways to become better, more well-rounded, and more effective human beings.

Rising to the occasion, one of the rising stars under my supervision picked learning to play the guitar and learning to tap dance as her personal improvement goals. Needless to say, our year-end evaluation conferences were more fun than most. We even drew an audience. Silly? Trivial? Foolish? Waste of time? All of the above? I don't think so.

The skills learned helped the staff member to better relate to the young people she served, boosted her self-confidence, strengthened our bond, introduced some fun into an often ominous process, and encouraged her to become an active player in the school's culture. Sometimes, lightening the tone is a worthy goal in itself. It can be empowering at the same time.

Occasionally, some people grow weary of empowerment. I once had an elementary principal tell me, "I don't want any more empowerment. I want someone to tell me what to do." Overall, empowerment is an overused term, yet an underused and undervalued culture-building tool.

Empowerment is a little risky. And scary. And unpredictable. Do it anyway. When school employees share in the power, they are no longer mere cogs in the culture; they are co-owners. I know lots of good teachers who would break down doors to work in a culture like that.

3. TRUST

The adhesive that bonds the organization together is trust. It is what makes the culture a culture, instead of an assortment of fragments.

Without the trust of your staff, you can't be a servant leader. In fact, you can't be a leader at all. You can only be a figurehead, a mouthpiece, a space filler, and a placeholder until a real leader comes to the rescue.

Like interest on an investment, trust has to be earned and takes time to build and compound. There are no shortcuts. You can't rush trust—or demand it, buy it, invent it, or get it over or under the counter. No matter how strong a leader you may be, you still have to pay your dues before you are admitted to the "trust club" of the organization.

How does a school leader go about earning the trust of teachers and other personnel? The old-fashioned way—by keeping promises, respecting confidentiality, treating everyone (no matter how high or low on the academic hierarchy) fairly and with respect and dignity, demonstrating loyalty, and telling the truth—all of it, not just an edited, scrubbed-up version.

Of course, the best way to build trust is to trust others. If you can't do that, don't count on becoming an effective school leader anytime soon.

Like all aspects of personal reputation, trust grows slowly but can erode quickly. Once you've earned it, guard it, nurture it, and protect it like a prized possession. Don't treat it lightly or take it for granted. The only thing more difficult than gaining the trust of your staff is regaining it should you lose it.

It is almost impossible to exaggerate the importance of trust to a healthy school environment. They define each other. When school personnel are asked what they want in a principal or superintendent, "trustworthiness" always comes out at or near the top. All school employees want a trusting relationship with their leaders. Without a foundation of trust, they won't buy into the culture of the organization. That's bad for everyone—especially the kids. Trust me.

4. CARING

If your staff knows or believes you care about kids, about public education, about what happens in the school, and about them, they will care too, and show it. But if they think you don't really care, they won't care either—and they will show it.

Caring counts. It is infectious and interactive. Caring enough can compensate for a host of lesser faults or failings.

But caring is an active verb. You can't just claim it, proclaim it, or announce it. You have to show it. You have to demonstrate how much you care through the accumulation of countless small gestures.

For example, after an unpleasant incident at school, Minneapolis superintendent Carol Johnson called principal Bernadela Johnson (no relation) at home to ask, "How are you? What do you need from us?" It's no wonder that Carol Johnson is recognized as one of the most caring school leaders on the planet.

Fortunately, there are as many ways to let your staff know how much you care as there are minutes in the school day. Effective leaders capitalize on every opportunity. My first piece of advice is, "Don't always wear a watch." Don't always be in a hurry.

Take time for people. Listen to them. Better yet, hear them out. Nothing says "I care" more than giving your full attention and actively listening.

Other powerful signals that you care include remembering the names of employees' family members and important events in their lives; holding more conversations than meetings; giving public expressions of appreciation; publicizing staff accomplishments; finding ways for teachers to share their good ideas (DVDs can help); being a cheerleader; offering verbal affirmations; admitting your own shortcomings; and sharing the blame for mistakes and the credit for successes.

It also helps to radiate confidence in your staff's ability and optimism about their chances for success. As Jane Hileman, CEO of America's Reading Promise, explains, a good leader must "be hope walking."

Most important, let staff members know you think they are doing a good job. It reinforces the sense of trust you have in them, and they will reciprocate.

Nothing feels much better than knowing your leader believes you are a good teacher (or custodian, or secretary). It is a lifelong spirit booster. If you can instill this feeling in your staff, you will not only attract the best, who will do their best, but you will also keep them for the long haul. That's how you build a lasting culture.

More than in businesses or many other organizations, the culture of a school is a function of the heart, as well as of the head. Remember, little children are involved. Feelings are important, and caring is imperative.

If you don't really care, don't bother to show up. No one will care if you don't.

5. LOYALTY

Loyalty is another lynchpin of a school culture that is staff-affirming. It simply means looking out for each other. Loyalty is the way the culture protects itself from itself and others.

My earliest recollection of the power of loyalty related to the group of friends I grew up with in a small Kansas community. Our little town didn't have many (okay—any) recreational facilities for young people, so we taught ourselves to swim in a nearby creek.

Then one summer, our community built a real public swimming pool, with diving boards and everything. We were ecstatic and counted the days until it opened. On opening day, we were lined up hours ahead of time.

But when the doors finally opened, a sad and unexpected thing occurred. One of our friends, a Mexican boy, was barred from entering. We didn't know the pool was segregated. We didn't even know what "segregated" meant. Naturally, our friend was embarrassed, mortified, and humiliated. The rest of us were stunned.

Although we had mixed emotions—we really wanted to swim in that brand-new pool—we all left together and went back to the creek to swim where everyone was welcome, and we had a good time.

Even little kids can have a culture, and loyalty is an integral part of the unwritten social contract.

Years later, as a grown-up, I've witnessed numerous similar gestures of loyalty, great and small, within school cultures, such as

- The case where a school board wanted to put a long-serving principal out to pasture to save money but the superintendent felt strongly that the principal deserved better treatment for his years of faithful service and said, "If he goes, I go." They both stayed.
- Or the experience of a district office administrator who was required by the school board to enter a treatment center for alcohol dependency. The official expected the board members to adopt a punitive posture or to distance themselves. Instead, the board sent flowers to his home as a gesture of loyalty, support, and good wishes for a successful recovery.
- Or the unusual, but true, story of a rookie teacher named Dan Jordan, who, in 1962, invited his students at George Washington High School in Denver, Colorado, to meet him on the first day of the new millennium (January 1, 2000) at the Denver Public Library and bring $1. Almost 40 years later, 300 students showed up on the right date, at the right place, with their dollars in hand. That's loyalty!
- Or the situation where the superintendent went against the best advice of his assistants (I was one of them) and appointed a very traditional principal, instead of a much more innovative candidate, to head up a new experimental, cutting-edge junior high school. "I respect your judgment," the superintendent told his advisers, "but I owe it to the principal who has stuck with me for many years." Sometimes, loyalty trumps logic. In this case, it worked out.

Obviously, there are more examples where these came from. You can probably think of even better ones. The point is that loyalty is not just a common feature of school cultures that accommodate staff needs; it is as necessary as oxygen. There is no culture without it.

6. COMMUNICATION

The life's blood of any successful school culture (or any culture) is communication. That's why Chapter 12 is devoted entirely to this subject. It's that important. Feel free to exercise patience or skip ahead—whatever suits your reading style.

All school cultures are different. But these six basic building blocks support the superstructure of successful cultures that satisfy, gratify, motivate, and inspire all staff members. The next obvious question is, "So what?"

If someone dumped a pile of building blocks on my driveway, I might know they were essential building materials, but I probably wouldn't know exactly what to do with them. I would need directions—some sort of plan or blueprint.

If you are like me, building blocks are not enough. In that case, the following action plan may help you get started putting the building blocks to use in creating a more staff-friendly school environment.

CREATING A MORE STAFF-FRIENDLY SCHOOL ENVIRONMENT

1. It All Starts With Hiring the Right People

It's true that there are no bad schools, only bad teachers, and that great teachers make a great culture.

That's why it pays to take time, every time, to do the hiring right. You're never just filling a position. You're changing the culture.

You want to hire staff members who are better than the existing culture. Business columnist Dale Dauten explains it this way: "The best managers spend little time managing, but a lot of time hiring. The secret is finding employees who don't need managing, ones with a standard higher than your own."

> *The employers usually get the employee they deserve.*
>
> —Sir Walter Bilby

How you hire people is a measure of your school's character. So is how you don't fire people. The best schools give all applicants and candidates some feedback. Every person who wants to work for you deserves a response, Yes or No. In many districts today, the only indication of rejection is silence. If you want your school culture to be known as a class act, you can do better. Some of these prospects may end up on your staff in the future. They deserve to be treated right, too.

Of course, finding the best people for what your culture expects or needs isn't easy; but there are tips that can help. Two of my favorite bits of hiring advice are:

- Read résumés from the bottom up. Any weaknesses are usually listed last.
- End every interview with this last question, "Is there anything else I should ask you?" It's a door opener that may reveal information that wouldn't surface otherwise.

Writer Isaac Cheifetz has also gleaned some insightful hiring hints from the experience of the National Football League's annual player draft, including:

- Look for a proven track record. Production trumps potential.
- Don't mistake eccentrics for jerks. Be open to hiring talented nonconformists.

- Don't make the mistake of thinking you can change people for the better or teach them passion or focus after you hire them. Or as Oprah Winfrey says, "When people show you who they are, believe them."

—————— ✂ ——————

Don't waste time trying to change ducks into eagles.

—Jim Rohn
motivational speaker

For many school leaders, it's just easier to ignore all the advice, make an educated guess (snap judgment), and get on with it. Don't fall into this trap. It's never smart to hurry through the hiring or to settle too soon.

Hiring is the first and most important thing you do in building a culture for the future. Always hire with the culture in mind, and do everything you can to get it right the first time.

2. Take the Hiring Initiative to the Next Level by Recruiting Tomorrow's Culture Builders Today

For a long time, experts have been telling us that the best way to assure quality teachers (especially minority teachers) in the future is to grow your own. Isn't it time we started listening?

If you're serious about building a world-class school culture for the long haul, why not start identifying talented prospective teachers while they are still in your schools? Then nurture and support them through high school, through college, and back into your schools as teachers themselves. The key is to convince benefactors to contribute to college scholarships and low-interest or no-interest student loans for qualified students who want to become teachers and are willing to return to the community as classroom teachers for a specified period of time.

Why not borrow a page from the popular, nationwide Breakthrough Programs (Breakthrough Kansas City, Breakthrough St. Paul, and so on) that allow interested high school– and college-age students (again, especially minorities) to explore their interest in teaching and to get an early taste of what teaching is like through firsthand experience working with students alongside regular teachers? If professional baseball can have farm clubs and a feeder system, why can't education?

Former students who return as teachers have the advantage of knowing the culture from the student's viewpoint and have a built-in bias in favor of the cultural views and mores embedded in the everyday life of the school. Homegrown teachers will probably be the biggest culture boosters you'll ever find.

More important, hiring them gives current staff members a sense that their investment in the culture has paid off. This makes cultivating in-house future culture builders a win-win situation. You don't run across these every day in this business.

3. Start Working to Strengthen and Sharpen the Connections Within the Culture

The quickest, easiest, and most effective way to make the school culture more user-friendly for staff members is to foster better connections and relationships among all the parties involved.

The goal should be to enhance existing connections and connect the dots where gaps exist. For starters, it helps to hold philosophical discussions on ethics and values to help move the participants toward consensus and a shared vision.

Other powerful steps to shore up internal connections are to exchange personal biographical sketches and to create opportunities for staff members to see each other in different roles and venues. Book clubs, investment groups, social events, retreats, sports teams, and volunteer community service projects are all effective "connecters."

4. Be Intentional About Jacking Up Staff Morale

Morale matters! How teachers and other personnel feel about themselves, their work, their boss, their school, and the future affects performance. High morale equals high productivity; and low morale translates into lackluster output.

That's why it's always a mistake to just let morale happen. It's always better to act, proact, react, or take whatever tack might move the dial of the "morale-o-meter" in a positive direction. The mere fact that you care enough to try to improve morale improves morale.

Other effective morale boosters include:

- Giving verbal "report cards"
- Sharing all the information that's worth knowing
- Being present and accessible
- Rotating good (and bad) assignments
- Writing personal notes of commendation and congratulation
- Setting aside a special "pride week" to celebrate each other and the positive aspects of the school culture. Popular pride week activities include secret pal gift exchanges, baby picture identification contest, progressive storytelling, and joint jigsaw puzzle solving.

It's not difficult to think of ways to help people feel better about where they are, who they're with, and what they do. The trick is to actually do some of them. You will be glad if you do. So will your staff.

5. Put a Lot of Your Eggs in the Staff Development Basket

Teachers love to grow. Learning is their life.

Of course, you often hear teachers say bad things about district training programs. That's because there are a lot of bad district training programs out there. Teachers resent workshops or inservice programs that are boring, overly theoretical, too obtuse, or too obvious or unrelated to what they do with children every day; but they love staff development experiences that are fresh, relevant, meaningful, practical, different, hands-on, interesting, exciting, and fun.

Teachers want learning opportunities that make them better teachers and give them information, skills, and ideas they can put to use in their classroom the next day. Teachers are eager to learn whatever makes them better and smarter and equips them to take on new, different, and greater challenges or responsibilities.

Some schools have had success introducing Problem-Based Learning (PBL) programs for teachers. It's an approach that meets all the criteria above. The idea is to have teachers learn by working alone and together to solve real-world school problems. This approach originated in the medical profession and is now becoming popular with educators and law enforcement personnel.

Give your teachers this kind of learning experience and you will not only have a better educational program for kids, you will also have good teachers climbing over the fence to get into your school culture. For many teachers—including some of the best—professional improvement is better than a pay raise.

It is also wise not to forget about or give up on sabbatical leaves for public school teachers. They're expensive, but they are also powerful incentives for serious, dedicated, ambitious professionals. If you can retain and maintain a viable schedule of sabbaticals, you will enrich your program for kids and endear yourself to the staff at the same time. That's creating a culture that works for everyone.

Some districts deal with the cost issue by taking advantage of matching dollars to create funds for sabbatical grants for teachers. Some philanthropists and corporate sponsors will offer matching monies to communities willing to raise the other funds necessary. It's worth some extra effort to pull off.

Of course, staff development, including sabbaticals, isn't for just the faculty. It's for everyone. All employees want, need, and deserve opportunities to grow and get better at what they do. Good cultures don't play favorites.

6. Make Mentorships One of Your Missions

Establish mentoring as the way you do business in your school. Encourage everyone to mentor or be mentored—or both.

When mentoring becomes the norm, you can be pretty certain that you have a helpful, welcoming, and supportive school culture. The beauty of mentorships is that they are reciprocal. They benefit both the mentor and the protégé and strengthen the overall culture at the same time. Parker J.

Palmer, founder of the Fetzer Institute Teacher Improvement Program, describes it well:

> Mentors and apprentices are partners in an ancient human dance. . . . It is the dance of the spiraling generations, in which the old empower the young with their experience and the young empower the old with new life, reweaving the fabric of the human community as they touch and turn.

Everyone needs a mentor (even mentors need mentors), because none of us is smart enough, informed enough, creative enough, brave enough, or strong enough to make it on our own. Sooner or later, all of us in education need advice, direction, instruction, and inspiration. And who couldn't use a good guide, role model, and cheerleader? That's where mentors come in.

My dictionary defines a mentor as "a wise and trusted counselor or teacher, especially in an occupational setting." You will do your school's culture a big favor if you ensure that everyone in the organization has access to such a "wise counselor."

Mentors give protégés what they need when they need it most and can't get it anywhere else, including knowledge, contacts, connections, resources, and reality checks. Effective mentors

- Teach what they don't teach in school.
- Open doors and point out pitfalls.
- Show how things really work.
- Reveal what's possible and support dreams.
- Challenge us to stretch beyond our comfort zone.
- Pick us up and prop us up as needed.
- Pump us up when we're deflated and deflate us when we're too full of ourselves.
- Give us permission to lighten up and laugh at ourselves—and laugh with us.
- Give us what others may not—the truth.

To achieve all these aims, mentors rely on many tools, such as modeling, direct teaching, positive reinforcement, role-playing, coaching, coaxing, cajoling, counseling, questioning, tough love, and listening. Of these, listening may be the most important. A good mentor just keeps listening until we give ourselves some good advice.

You can promote mentoring within your school community by emphasizing

- That you are never too old or experienced to need a mentor. (I even know educators who have hooked up with new mentors after retirement.)
- That mentors can come from anywhere, including businesses and other professions. Mentors can cross-pollinate.
- That mentors don't have to be older than their protégés. (I've mentored several younger protégés who ended up mentoring me.)

Another way to boost mentoring is to clarify the roles. For example, John R. Hoyle, leadership specialist from Texas A&M University, suggests the Mentor's Creed excerpted below:

Mentor's Creed

To set the right example for your protégé by your actions.

To be consistent in your temperament . . .

To be fair, impartial and consistent . . .

To show a sincere, personal interest in your protégés . . .

To be appreciative of your protégés' efforts and generous in praise . . .

To use every opportunity to teach your protégés how to do their job better . . .

To show your protégés that you can "do" as well as "manage" by pitching in to work beside them when help is needed.

—Author unknown

Obviously, I'm a big fan of mentoring, because mentors are culture brokers. They introduce and interpret the culture to newcomers and make everyone more effective in the process. If you can infuse a tradition of mentoring into the culture of the organization, your school will be a better place for teachers to teach and for kids to learn. That makes you a hero.

7. Create a Culture of Innovation

It energizes and enlivens the organization and makes it more fun to come to work. Better yet, innovation is a magnet for talent. Many of the best teachers like to be pioneers and pathfinders and part of a creative environment.

The first step is to convince the staff that you truly are open to different approaches and willing to give good new ideas a chance. It's true that great ideas can come from anywhere; but many of the best ideas already exist within the culture of your school—inside someone's head. But it's not enough just to encourage staff members to innovate. You have to persuade them that it's safe to let their ideas out and that good suggestions will get a fair hearing.

The best way to start is to implement a multifaceted approach to seeking and soliciting suggestions. A single "suggestion box" is not sufficient.

Some schools have had success creating an "innovation station" Web site where teachers can share their best practices and propose new ways of doing things. It also helps to allow teams of teachers to propose changes and innovations.

Of course, the acid test is whether or not you actually do something with the sound ideas you receive. Don't ask for ideas if you're not ready, willing, or able to act. Some principals and superintendents are like a dog chasing a car. If they ever caught a good idea, they wouldn't know what to do with it.

But the best school leaders know a good idea when they see it, give preference to ideas that will actually improve student achievement, reward ideas that have merit by putting them into practice, and, once approved, give each innovation the time, resources, and encouragement it needs to succeed—or fail—on its own.

Inventiveness is a sign of a vibrant culture. Lack of it may indicate a fossilized culture. The leader sets the tone. You're the leader. It's your call.

8. Initiate a Program of "Teaching Coaches"

Even champions need coaches. So why not offer coaching assistance to your champions—the school's classroom teachers?

The idea is to provide a qualified coach who will observe classroom instruction (at the invitation of the teacher) and offer pointers for improvement in a nonthreatening way.

Coaches may offer assistance with discipline problems, classroom management, teaching techniques, or organizational issues by providing feedback, advising, demonstrating, or just listening.

Some schools use graduate students as coaches. (For example, the University of Kansas offers middle school coaches who are experienced teachers with a proven track record of successful teaching.) Other schools use regular staff members who have become trained observers as part of an alternative career compensation program.

Teaching coaches offer a concrete approach to breaking down the sense of isolation (that "sink or swim on your own" feeling) that many young teachers experience. The message is that it is socially acceptable within the mores of the school culture to admit the need for help and, more important, that help is available.

9. Recognize Outstanding Performance With Noncash, Symbolic Rewards

Public schools don't give bonuses, but they can give recognition awards.

Actually, research in the psychology of motivation indicates that symbolic awards work as well or better than cash as employee incentives—particularly in caring professions such as education. These awards are especially effective when given in a timely manner, rather than waiting until the end of the year.

For example, I used to work with a school that gave out Pathfinder Awards for outstanding teaching and Asset Builder Awards for exemplary efforts to nurture developmental assets in young people. (Incidentally, a custodian was the first recipient of the Asset Builder Award.)

You probably have similar awards in your school. If not, you should. They work. In a culture where peers recognize peers, people try harder, good performance is validated, and job satisfaction is increased. Now that is a culture that works for the staff, as well as for the students.

10. Invest in the Culture

Remember the old admonition, "Put your money where your mouth is"? It's not just idle palaver. It's a basic principle of leadership.

Budgets are always tight. There are always lots of demands for the school's limited funds. Effective school leaders see to it that some money is earmarked to improve the school environment.

The values-driven Medtronic Corporation makes available "Quest Grants" of up to $50,000 to allow employees to try out some of their pet, far-out ideas for improvement. It is part of the corporate culture to support employee "creative freedom."

Of course, unless your school recently won the lottery, you may not have an extra $50,000 to spread around; but you and I both know that you could find a modest amount of seed money for improvement projects if you wanted to badly enough.

I'm reminded of a superintendent—in a district experiencing hard times and annual budget cutbacks—who continued to insist that some money be set aside each year for "enhancements" to the school's culture. It was his way of demonstrating that even in bad times there are still possibilities for making things better. His creative budgeting kept a spirit of hope alive during troubled times.

Somehow, leaders can always discover a little money for what they feel is most important. Sometimes, it is a matter of prioritization or trade-offs. Enlarging the car allowance for administrators may not improve the culture, but paying to transport some low-income students to a concert may. Likewise, paying for school board members to attend a national convention may not be a culture builder, but paying for more students to attend summer school or paying to send some teachers to a reading conference may be. Sometimes, buying more tests won't help the culture as much as purchasing new math texts. The point is that, whenever possible, budget decisions should reflect the values of the school culture. Let's face it: money talks. If you use some of your school's money to make a statement about what's important to a healthy school environment, people will listen.

11. Eliminate Second-Class Citizenship Within Your School Culture

Teachers may have degrees and licenses and get paid more; but try running a school without clerical personnel, custodians, technicians, aides, or bus drivers.

Teachers don't have a monopoly on compassion for kids, passion for their work, specialized expertise, or commitment to excellence. The staff has many components. All are important. Don't allow some segments of the school staff to feel put down, excluded, slighted, or relegated to second-class status.

How can you level the playing field? Start by including representatives of all staff categories in policy meetings and on important school committees. After all, custodians know a thing or two about discipline problems in the school. And receptionists know more than anyone what parents and the public are complaining about. Likewise, bus drivers often know better than teachers what kids are buzzing about. The culture works for all staff members only when all staff members are invited to the table.

Other ways to become more inclusive are to spend time with all employee groups (listen to what they're proud of—and what they complain about), offer all staff members professional growth and training opportunities and career advancement paths, and give awards for peak performance in all spheres of the school's operation.

If some members of your school team feel unimportant, you're doing something wrong. It's your job to make sure that everyone's contributions are recognized and appreciated.

12. Give Teachers Permission to Go Beyond No Child Left Behind (NCLB)

If all your school does is meet the standards of NCLB legislation, you are shortchanging students, staff, and the community.

There is more—much more—to an education than passing tests based on minimum standards. Besides, teachers hate teaching to tests. It makes them feel used, demeaned, and deprived of the opportunity to use all their gifts.

Encourage—no, better than that—*insist* that your teachers teach more than canned content and test-taking skills. Give them extra credit for dreaming. Support them in getting to know children's individual needs, teaching thinking skills, providing basic character education, and inspiring students to exceed expectations.

You can't fatten the cattle merely by weighing them.

—Author unknown

If you want your school to be the best it can be, strive for a culture that leaves No Child Left Behind far behind.

The dozen measures above are just a few of the action steps that can lead to a more accommodating culture for staff members. Obviously, there are many more, including all the usual suspects, such as flattening the bureaucracy, reducing red tape, and breaking down physical, political, and cultural barriers. Since every situation is unique, you are in the best position to determine what else is needed in your school to create an environment where all staff members thrive.

Some skeptics may wonder, Why all the fuss? If school is for kids, why worry so much about creating an internal environment that is comfortable and appealing to the staff? The doubters miss the point. That's kind of like saying, "Who cares if the doctor is sick? He's not the patient."

The goal isn't to pamper the staff or turn the school into a Club Med or country club for teachers. Rather, the aim is to provide a setting that capitalizes on all the assets of the staff and uses all their gifts to benefit students.

On a commercial plane flight, if there is trouble and the oxygen masks come down, the first bit of advice is always to put on your own mask before attempting to help children put on their masks. In other words, take care of yourself first, so you are better able to help others. That's what this whole "building a culture that works for staff" business is all about. As leader of the school, if you take good care of your staff, they will take good care of you, and, more important, they will take good care of kids. It's that servant leader thing in action.

And as mentioned earlier, an important side effect of creating a staff-friendly school culture is that it attracts winners. Great teachers gravitate to a school where they connect with the culture. An empowering, supportive environment not only attracts the best teachers but also keeps them—sometimes even after retirement.

For example, retirees at the Hale Community School in Minneapolis keep coming back years after retirement to help out in a remedial reading lab for students who have fallen behind in fluency and comprehension. Retirees run the lab every day and recruit other retired teachers to help out as well. As Candyce Ihnot, one of the retired Hale teachers, explained, "At other schools, teachers walk out and never want to come back. When we retired, we still wanted to be here, which really says something about the school setting." When you hear your retired teachers talk like that, you will know you have created a school culture that makes good teaching both possible and probable.

Famed anthropologist Margaret Mead once defined the ideal culture as one in which there was a place for every human gift. I won't even attempt to improve on Margaret Mead. She wasn't talking specifically about school cultures, but she could have been. Make your school a place where every staff member's gifts are noticed, nurtured, and utilized to the fullest and you will have earned another Servant Leader's Merit Badge.

But you're not done yet. There is more to the equation for a fully functioning school culture that boosts achievement and works for everyone. If you leave out parents and the community, the formula is incomplete. After all, a school and its culture can be only as strong as the community allows it to be. That's why Chapter 10 shows how to factor the entire community into the education equation.

10

The Dancing Bear Metaphor

Creating a School Culture That Works for Parents and the Community

A school system without parents at its foundation is just like a bucket with a hole in it.

—Rev. Jesse Jackson, civil rights activist

Many principals and teachers see their schools as castles under constant attacks by barbarian taxpayers and savage journalists . . . they're defensive. And they're not about to discuss what's wrong with the drawbridge or admit that the moat has run dry.

—Joanne Jacobs, author of *Our School* (2005)

———————————— ✧ ————————————

Once upon a time, the school could be a little arrogant, aloof, and distant from parents and the community. It could look down and talk down to the public and get away with it.

People were in awe of educational institutions. They respected public school teachers—and even called them "professor." If the teacher punished the child at school, the parents punished the child at home. No questions asked.

There was a time when parents dressed up to go to a conference with their child's teacher. A time when the school literally could do no wrong. There was also a time when gasoline cost 25 cents a gallon; but that doesn't have much to do with today's world. Today, things are different.

People bad-mouth, question, and criticize their public schools and blame teachers for much of what's wrong with society. They call teachers lots of things—but "professor" isn't one of them. People argue with teachers today. They harass teachers. They sue teachers. Sometimes, they even shoot teachers.

The public doesn't blindly believe everything the school teaches and preaches anymore. Some even call the curriculum subversive or un-American. Columnists have even been known to label teachers' unions as "terrorist organizations."

Today, parents have choices. If they don't like one school, they switch to another. A growing number just keep their kids home, because they think they can do a better job of educating their children than the school can. What a difference a few decades make!

What does all this mean for you and me? Simply, that the school—your school and mine—can no longer be removed or remote from the rest of the community. The same sensitivity used to shape the culture internally must now be applied to other stakeholders outside of the school.

The school can't act as if it is somehow superior to the general public. To succeed today, the school has to be an integral part of the community. And the community has to be part of the school. It's the only way either can survive.

No culture has a monopoly on goodness and common sense.

—Mary Pipher
psychologist and author

The school has the power to open up the community, while the community has the power to close down the school. My former superintendent, Carl Holmstrom, had it right: "The school works only when the partnership (between the school and the community) works."

That's why the culture of the school has to include and work for parents and the entire community, or it doesn't work at all. When the school's culture and the community's values, priorities, rules, and expectations are at odds, kids are caught in the middle and gridlock replaces education. When the two cultures are in sync, stand back and make room—wonderful things are about to happen for children.

Of course, the school has to rely on the parents and community members for their customers, resources, moral support, lobbying, direction, wisdom, values, volunteers, and validation. Most important, the community holds the purse strings. At the same time, the community—any community—is emotionally bankrupt without the energy, the renewal, the hope, and the future that only the school can provide.

Of course, there are still plenty of teachers, and even some administrators, who don't want to let the community get too close. They would like to lock the doors to keep out pushy parents, media meddlers, and nosy critics. Some even try it. These are the same teachers who don't want visitors and volunteers clut-

When the school is closed, the entire community seems empty.

—Author unknown

tering up their classroom space. You probably have a few of these people on your staff at this very moment. But they are a dying breed. They just don't realize that they are waiting to become extinct.

If you want to be a successful school leader today, avoid the isolationists, Luddites, and separatists like the plague! And start learning how to work for and with the entire community. There simply is no weasel room, wiggle room, or elbow room anymore. You have to include the public and engage the whole community in the affairs of the school. Or fail. But before you start, there is one caution—and it's a whopper. It's called the "Dancing Bear Metaphor."

Like many people, I first heard this forewarning from Jim Brimeyer, the only public servant I've ever known who has worked both sides of the street as a hired city manager and, later, as an elected city council member in the same city. As Brimeyer explains, "When you teach a bear to dance, you had better be ready to keep dancing until the bear decides to quit."

You can't open the school to parents and the community members half time, part-time, or temporarily. It's not an ad hoc deal. You have to be prepared to stick with it for the long haul.

Once citizens get a taste of meaningful involvement (e.g., serving as site council members, classroom volunteers, or advisory committee representatives), they are not going to be willing to back off. They won't be content to sit on the sidelines—on the outside, looking in—ever again. Once you invite the public to the dance, you have to keep dancing until the ball is over. You can't take it back. Or uninvite the public. Your dance partners won't let you quit.

There is another caveat. Building a school culture that works for parents and the community takes time—a lot of time. It is a lengthy, unhurried process of earning trust, discovering and defining a shared passion, finding common ground, arriving at consensus, testing limits, and negotiating boundaries. Patience is the tool of choice in constructing a shared culture. Some principals and superintendents don't get it right, because they rush the process, skip a few steps, or don't take enough time.

Some observers compare the process to what happens in the Afghan culture, where it takes three cups of tea to do business. On the first cup, you are a stranger. With the second cup, you become a friend. With the third cup, you become family. But the process takes years.

Interfacing and integrating the cultures of the school and the community are a lot like that. As with fine tea, you have to allow time for relationships to steep in order to become rich, mellow, and full-bodied. Patience isn't only a virtue for effective school leaders—it's a cultural imperative.

Despite the difficulties, one phenomenon that eases the alignment of the school's and the community's cultures is that they usually have more similarities than differences. Research on community development at Northwestern University has identified certain assets necessary for a vital community: individual skills and talents, associations and networks, professional expertise, physical resources, and economic resources. You guessed it: these are the same basic ingredients for a vital school environment. The real pros work on the similarities and the shared assets to overcome the differences.

As mentioned earlier, school personnel cannot return to the past or reinvent it; but they can learn important lessons from particles of the past. We all know adults who—not so long ago—grew up in small towns or rural areas and can recall when the school was the heart of the entire community and the hub of communal activity. It was more than a place of learning; it was a gathering place, a showcase for cultural and artistic pursuits, a sports venue, and an entertainment center for all ages. The school provided a source of learning, social cohesion, stability, and continuity.

It was everybody's school. Everyone—young and old—supported the school, felt a part of it, and took pride in it. The school was an integral piece of the culture of the community. Likewise, the community was an integral component of the culture of the school. They were a seamless, unified force.

If you ask people from this background, most will attest that having mutually supportive school and community cultures created a rich, fear-free, nurturing atmosphere for kids that made it easier to achieve, excel, and fulfill individual potential.

Can such an integration of school and community cultures exist today? In a big city? In a sprawling suburb? In a merged, consolidated, amalgamated, hybrid rural school area? The most obvious (and truthful) answer is No. Not completely; but it can come close.

Even in today's diverse, polarized, and fragmented society, reinforcing cultures can be found in pockets of schools and communities of all sizes across the country. Wherever they exist, they establish an old-fashioned sense of belonging and a positive milieu for teaching, learning, growing, and achieving.

If this sounds like something you want for your students, staff, parents, and community at large, it can happen. You can help make it happen. It all starts with the parents—by giving them what they need and putting their assets to work to make the school better for everyone.

Parents deserve special attention. After all, unless you screw it up, they are your school's most empathetic and knowledgeable partners. Parents and school personnel not only share the same children, but they also share the same goals for those children.

That should make it easy to incorporate parents into the culture of the school. Unfortunately, some educators have an undeniable talent for muddying the water, complicating simplicity, obscuring the obvious, and transforming the easy into the incredibly difficult.

The key to enlisting maximum parental interest, active involvement, support, and cooperation lies in the school's attitude toward parents. How the staff perceives parents is a deal maker or deal breaker. There is a direct linear relationship between attitude and action and reaction. The school staff's attitude toward parents determines how they treat parents, which defines the parents' behavior toward the school. (Does the term "the Golden Rule" fit in here somewhere?)

A negative attitude toward parents makes them quick to judge and criticize and can lead to excessive backbiting, labeling, stereotyping, and profiling. If this kind of negative attitude is part of your school culture, don't count on much help from parents—or anyone else.

If you want to drive away parents in droves or give them a severe case of Intermittent Explosive Disorder, adopt a patronizing or condescending attitude. Or an air of suspicion or paranoia. Or worse yet, an attitude of smug superiority. Don't act as if you know more about their children than the parents themselves know. You don't.

The best way to gauge your staff's attitude toward parents is simply to listen to what they say about parents in the teachers' lounge or over coffee after school, when no parents or students are around. You probably should listen to yourself as well.

What the school staff says about parents and how they say it reveals what they really think and feel. Trash talk can help entrench a negative attitude toward parents within the school environment. Saying stupid or mean-spirited stuff about parents doesn't make it true—but it does make it part of the school's culture.

What works best is an attitude that values, appreciates, and respects parents and the difficult choices they have to make every day. It pays to remember that parents are the school's voice and first line of defense in the community. They can and should be the school's first and foremost liaisons, advocates, buffers, supporters, interpreters, cheerleaders, and lobbyists. Parents can be the school's best friend. Or its worst enemy. If parents become your school's enemy, it's not their fault. It's yours.

It is absolutely imperative that parents believe in the school. If they don't, nothing else matters very much. You can't have a viable, effective culture without them.

Building parents into the culture of the school often starts even before their students are enrolled in your school. You can't keep good students and good families in your school unless you get them enrolled in the first place. I'm reminded of some Catholic friends of mine who were trying to decide whether to enroll their first child in public or parochial school. As part of the decision-making process, they took their child to the local public school kindergarten round-up.

Immediately upon entering, they were asked to complete a registration form. They explained that they hadn't decided on enrolling yet and were just visiting. The clerk handling the paperwork exclaimed, "You have to come to this school. You don't have a choice." My friends countered, "Yes, we do have a choice. We're considering private schools as well."

The crestfallen clerk was at a loss about what to do. She finally told them that since they weren't registering, their child couldn't get an identification tag, which was to be used to group students for a tour of the school and an opportunity to meet the teachers. No registration . . . No tag . . . No tour . . . Period. Later, while all the other children went off to explore the school, my friend's little boy had to remain behind in the auditorium with the adults.

This unwelcoming experience pretty much made the school choice decision for my friends. Their child didn't enroll in the public school. Neither did his three brothers who came along later. In one brief, thoughtless encounter, the school lost not just one potential student but four.

In this real-life vignette, there was no intentional slight, malice, or discrimination. Just clumsy handling of an unexpected situation and failure to be prepared or flexible enough to handle an unforeseen contingency. The culture wars are won or lost over brief skirmishes like this. The moral of this tale is that successful culture building requires starting early, paying attention to detail, and being courageous enough to bend silly rules when appropriate.

Once they are officially part of your organization, the quickest, easiest, and best way to solidify the parents' place in the culture is to increase their physical presence in the school. The winning schools today are parent-participation schools. That's why effective principals and superintendents encourage massive parent volunteerism.

Using lots of parent volunteers provides much-needed extra hands and heads to help the staff, and makes the parents more staunch advocates of the school at the same time. What's not to like about that?

Where volunteer programs work best, the school has a parent volunteer coordinator (who can also be a volunteer), insists on giving volunteers meaningful tasks (not mindless, made-up work), and is mindful of the politics of volunteering (e.g., some parents volunteer primarily to "puff themselves up" and to gain preferential treatment for their children and themselves).

In addition to showcasing volunteer opportunities, other effective ways to make the school work for all parents include the following:

1. Offer workshops on parenting skills and issues. The more the school can help parents do their job better, the better able parents are to support and assist the school in its job.

2. Make home visits the way every teacher does business in your school. Startle yourself. Find out how great a difference home visits can make. But remember the Dancing Bear Metaphor. Once you start visiting students and parents on their home turf, you can't decide to stop abruptly.

3. Become a "no report card school." Instead, provide parents with on-demand, online information about their child's progress. Parents can help their student and the school more when they have access to their child's grades (and other information) anytime they want it.

4. Make things simple and hassle-free for parents. You may have heard about the Chicago school system's adoption of a Dropout Consent Form. Huh?

In an effort to teach better decision making, Chicago became the first and only system in the nation to require dropouts and their parents to sign a consent form, which warned of the possible pitfalls of quitting school, such as unemployment and possible jail sentences.

It was a move that ranks at the top of the chart for Stupid Educators' Tricks. In the first place, most students quitting school don't formally resign. They just stop showing up. Second, the form represents a typical, mindless bureaucratic response to a problem: create more paperwork.

Avoid creating more paperwork, levels of approval, or other road-blocks for your parents. Removing obstacles is leadership. Creating obstacles is antileadership. Your school doesn't need more forms. It needs easier access for parents to all the help they need when they need it. Keep things simple. What could be simpler than that?

5. Meet the special needs of special groups of parents within your school. One of the best examples I know of is teaching English to the parents of English Language Learner (ELL) students.

6. Communicate with parents regularly and in understandable terms. No jargon. No educationese. No nonsense. No kidding.

The bottom line is that anything you can do to make parents feel more comfortable with the school, feel more welcome and at home in the school, and feel like a valued contributor to the school boosts the odds of parents becoming a functional part of the school culture.

It doesn't take any elaborate measures, costly add-ons, or fancy foot-work to engage parents positively in the school. It just takes common sense.

The secret is to treat parents as insiders. And give them some slack. Remember that "when it's your own kid, it's different." Parents are completely logical, rational, and sensible human beings—except when their own child is involved. Accept this. If you are a parent, you are the same way. That's why an understanding, sympathetic, and supporting attitude will win parents over every time.

Of course, even if you win over every parent in town, that's not enough. There's more? You bet! Parents are just the base. Your school's culture isn't complete until it works for the entire community. Today, it doesn't just take a whole village to raise a child; it takes a whole village to run an effective school. That means the cultures of the school and the community have to both supplement and complement each other.

How do they do that? Through the accumulation of countless small acts that bind the fortunes and the futures of the school and the community together.

Since examples are better than diatribes, following is a treasury of down-to-earth ways the school can link with the community and vice versa. These stratagems represent the nitty-gritty grunt work of culture building.

If you don't find something you, your school, or your community can use among these suggestions, you may be perfect already. Stop reading and start helping the rest of us achieve nirvana.

Linking the Community to the School (Samples and Examples)

- Create opportunities for adults in the community to listen to students talk about their concerns, accomplishments, dreams, problems, fears, and ideas for the future. An annual Mayor's Youth Summit has proved to be a valuable forum for youth in many communities.
- Organize neighborhoods to support students (e.g., identify "safe homes," monitor school bus stops, and turn on lights during winter months when students are coming home at dusk).
- Sponsor a "Caring Tree" drive, where people can donate school supplies to help low-income students get off to a head start on the school year.
- Hold an annual Caring Youth Recognition event to honor students who give back to the community,
- Create performance venues and opportunities for student groups—both formal school groups (e.g., band, orchestra, chorus) and freelance groups (e.g., garage bands).
- Form community booster clubs to support athletic teams and other school groups and activities. (Note: there is a difference between boosters and boasters.)
- Establish a free clinic for teens and low-income families staffed by volunteer physicians and nurses.
- Collect used instruments for use by low-income music students.
- Encourage local businesses to adopt a school.
- Establish a local nonprofit public school foundation to raise funds to support school programs.

- Open a "Kids' Café" to provide healthy evening meals for low-income kids and families. Arrange for students to earn and learn by working in the café as meal planners, cooks, servers, and clean-up staff.
- Organize a "Day One" program to welcome students back to school on the first day and to celebrate the youth of the community.
- Encourage local corporations to fund programs to prepare minority and low-income students for college. The Medtronic Corporation's "Admission Possible" program is a good example.
- Introduce a communitywide reading project to get all ages reading the same book at the same time. The program I'm most familiar with adopted the motto, "Make a good book better—read it together," and sponsored a variety of events and activities to bring whole families together around a shared reading experience, encourage intergenerational connections, and build community unity.
- Form an intergenerational theater group. One community I've read about sponsors an annual event where mixed-age teams write, rehearse, and perform a play within 24 hours.
- Allow kids to participate in community decision making (e.g., planning biking and hiking trails, serving on city committees and commissions, and participating in local visioning and strategic planning exercises).
- Encourage local merchants to treat student customers with respect, instead of suspicion.
- Recruit local adult musicians to sit in and play along with junior and senior bands and orchestras.
- Make family time a community priority. Repeated studies show that students have fewer problems and do better in school when their families spend time together on a regular basis. Some communities have introduced "Eat, Talk, Connect" programs where families commit to eat three meals together each week. Others have set aside "family nights" where participating organizations agree to ban scheduled events, practices, games, or homework so families can hang out together. Still other communities go "unplugged" for an occasional evening when no TV, computer, cell phone, or iPod use is allowed, and the time is devoted to family activities. Any effort to strengthen families helps kids succeed in school and builds a healthier community at the same time.
- Bring local clergy together to draft a common set of "core values" essential to a wholesome environment for the children in the community. Clergy from different religions and denominations agree? On something? On anything? Sound impossible? It's not. It happened with the faith community in my town. And it can happen in yours.

I know. I know. It's a long list. It could be much longer. There is no cap on the number of ways for the community to connect with the school. The more frequent and numerous the connections, the stronger the cultures of both the school and the community become.

Connecting should be reciprocal. The school can't just passively keep taking support, encouragement, assistance, and resources from the community. It has to reciprocate, reach out, repay, and reconnect with the community at large.

One of the first steps is to ensure accessibility—to make it easy for parents and community members to contact appropriate school officials or other personnel when they need and want answers or assistance. Technology can help. Or hinder.

For example, when one school district I knew first replaced its human switchboard operator with an automated answering system, callers were confronted with a simple menu:

For Payroll, press one

For Accounts Payable, press two

For Purchasing, press three

For Maintenance, press four

That's it. Nothing else. I don't want to say this qualifies as a Stupid Educators' Trick, but you decide. None of the menu choices identified contacts most parents and other callers were interested in. Most callers want to talk to the superintendent's office, an individual school, the special education department, the curriculum offices, or human resources—not purchasing or payroll.

It should come as no surprise that the answering system was quickly replaced. Now the district has gone back to a human answering system. Sometimes, the human touch still trumps technology in culture building.

Besides ensuring hassle-free availability and accessibility, there are countless other opportunities for the school to connect with community members in ways that benefit the community, the students, and the school at the same time. Here's how some successful schools do it.

Linking the School to the Community (Samples and Examples)

- Try holding principal's office hours in a local coffee shop, or scheduling "Soup With the Sup" lunch sessions, where citizens can get to know the superintendent up close and personal.
- Identify a school district ombudsman as the go-to person for straight answers about the schools. Where such positions already exist, the ombudsman typically investigates concerns and answers questions about

school policy, procedures, curriculum, discipline, staffing, and school assignments. Some people mistakenly assume that an ombudsman is supposed to be an advocate for students and parents. Actually, a good ombudsman is primarily a seeker of truth.

- Assign students to collect oral histories from senior citizens and to interview immigrants on video. The students from one school even wrote a song honoring the wisdom of the community's elders. In another district, students created a traveling display featuring the stories of local immigrant students, including why they came here, how they came, what obstacles they overcame, what they brought with them, and what they had to leave behind.

- Sponsor a Chore Day when athletic teams and other student groups perform chores for senior citizens and others in the community who need help.

- Use students to train Little League and other community sports team coaches on how to be good role models for kids.

- Initiate intergenerational activities involving high school students and senior citizens. Actually, teenagers and seniors have a lot in common. (For example, people hesitate to give them serious responsibilities, think they dress and talk funny, worry about them driving, and are uncomfortable with them having sex.) That makes the two groups natural allies. They can learn a lot from each other. And have fun together at the same time. One community even named their intergenerational program JOY (Joining Old and Younger).

- Develop positive working relationships with local private and parochial schools. Invite these schools to your district's "School Choice Fair." Some public school parents may be enticed by the private school programs; likewise, some private school parents may see something they like in the public schools. After all, the most important consideration should be to find the best fit for every child. The entire community can also benefit from cooperative projects and initiatives that the public and private schools undertake together. Examples include shared facilities, cooperative fundraising, charity drives and service projects, and joint celebrations and performances. Public and private schools share too many common goals to settle for being merely competitors or rivals. The community's public and private schools are just different faces of education for kids.

- Encourage school athletic teams to show appreciation to the community. For example, after every 2004–2005 basketball game in Braham, Minnesota, the entire undefeated, state champion team gathered in the gym lobby to thank parents, patrons, family members, and anyone else in attendance for coming to watch the game. Try it. It's guaranteed to knock the socks off your local fans and generate more goodwill than you could buy with a year's public relations budget.

After reading this list, if all this community courting seems like too much work, you don't have to do it. You can still operate in a vacuum—isolated and insulated from outsiders—just as earlier educational life forms once did. The only minor drawback is that your school culture will become increasingly smug, self-serving, self-protective, self-righteous, cautious, defensive, paranoid, and, eventually, irrelevant.

Many of us have observed once-popular schools that no one takes seriously anymore. They've become inbred and disconnected from the community. They've outlived their usefulness. They no longer want to dance with the bear, so the bear dances on ahead without them.

In the real world, your school is absolutely dependent on the community for acceptance and support. Just as every nation must learn to be a global participant today, every school has to learn to become part of the broader community.

Teachers in the twenty-first century will be "village builders."

—Hank Rubin, educator-author

The best possible scenario for kids . . . and for staff . . . and for parents . . . and, in fact, for everyone is when the culture of the school and the culture of the community overlap, sharing the same goals, core values, priorities, and preferred processes. When the lines separating the two cultures become blurred, everyone wins.

Of course, it's hard work. Winning at anything is difficult and demanding. What makes it even more challenging is that there are myriad options and opportunities for the school to link up with the community, as shown above—and the best school leaders take advantage of as many as possible. Despite the multiple possibilities, the undergirding principles for making the school culture work for parents and the overall community are few and simple.

Successful retailers have always known what it takes to win clients and customers, including

- A superior product
- Top-notch, courteous, customer-friendly service
- Good value
- Knowledgeable and helpful staff members

Wouldn't you know! These are the same principles it takes to win over parents and community members. Without these elements, the community can quickly lose interest and quit buying what the school is selling. Just as in retailing, your challenge is to be accountable and prove to the community and the world that your school delivers what it promises.

If you can do that, you will have more than a school environment that works for everyone. You will have what all the reformers are clamoring for—*results!* Read on.

11

A Results-Oriented Work Environment (ROWE)

Linking Culture and Achievement

School cultures, in short, are key for school achievement and student learning.

> —Terrence Deal and Kent Peterson, educators
> and authors of *Shaping School Culture* (1999)

The great law of culture: Let each become all that he was created capable to become.

> —Thomas Carlyle, British historian and essayist

———————— ✖ ————————

Does the culture of the organization drive student success? Does environment affect performance? Does a positive school culture boost achievement? Do students like summer vacation?

If you've read this far, you should know that the culture of the school absolutely influences student success (or failure). More than anything else, it can elevate achievement or depress performance. Culture is a bigger factor in shaping student achievement than the school budget, the curriculum, the textbooks, the teaching techniques, or perhaps even heredity.

If you want better grades, higher test scores, or better graduation rates, create a better learning environment—one that allows the budget, the curriculum, the textbooks, and the teaching techniques to do their job. Culture and achievement are forever linked.

That's why if we (you and I) wanted to, we could create a school culture in which virtually every child fails. Of course, we don't want to—but we could. We could foster an environment so toxic, hostile, and oppressive that learning would be next to impossible.

We would build it out of low or no expectations, artificially high standards, negative attitudes, fear, intimidation, humiliation, coercion, impersonality, and lots and lots of rules. Fortunately, we don't want to. We want to build a culture where every child has a shot at success. We can do that, too.

In the business world, major corporations, such as Best Buy, talk about creating a Results-Oriented Work Environment—an atmosphere that gets things done—that meets expectations, delivers on promises, and produces desired outcomes. The company gives it the acronym ROWE.

At Best Buy, the only requirement for a ROWE is to get the job done, whether it takes 24 hours or 40 hours; and the only evaluative measure of success is, Did it get done?

Schools aren't businesses. They're more. What students, teachers, administrators, parents, school boards, taxpayers, legislators, critics, and reformers all want for their schools is the same thing Best Buy wants—*results!*

How can Best Buy and the schools get what they want? Simply by creating an environment that is conducive to peak performances.

Have you seen the comedic Cable Guy on TV whose mantra is "Git 'r Done"? That's exactly what a positive school culture that brings out the best in everyone will do for you. It will Git 'r Done.

Unfortunately, there are still people who think devoting time, attention, and effort to developing a positive culture is a waste of time. They view culture building as just so much touchy-feely, namby-pamby, bleeding-heart, self-esteemy hogwash. They want a no-nonsense, no-excuses, no-let-up, no-mercy, no-prisoners education. Sometimes, they don't realize that this is a form of school culture in itself. Truthfully, I sometimes wish they would get what they want and that their children would have to live with it. Then again, I wouldn't really want to wish this fate on any kids.

I can't even begin to find words strong enough, direct enough, critical enough, hard-hitting enough, or eloquent enough to express adequately just how incredibly wrong and misguided these people are. If I had strong feelings on the subject, I'd tell you how I really feel about this. Here's a hint: it has something to do with teaching the canaries not to sing.

School administrators may do some things that waste time foolishly. The time they spend on building a proper teaching-learning environment isn't one of them. Nothing influences student success more than the educational ethos of the school. In fact, achievement is largely the self-fulfilling prophecy of a healthy school culture.

Let the terminally hard-nosed waste time dragging out their whips and chains and overweight rulebooks. Real leaders spend their time more effectively by removing obstacles and motivating and empowering teachers to teach and learners to learn.

Of course, culture isn't everything. Ability always plays a role in success. Bright kids tend to do pretty well in almost any culture—but they could do even better in a more affirming atmosphere. Besides, achievement isn't just for the smart kids. Given the right environment, all students can achieve!

That's why a teacher at Claremont High School in San Diego, California, started the AVID Foundation. AVID stands for Achievement Via Individual Determination. The AVID Foundation's philosophy is that kids are smarter than they think they are—and even smarter than most people and even many educators think they are.

AVID encourages marginal students to take more difficult courses, rather than easier, watered-down, or remedial programs. The foundation's explanation is that "Hard work makes kids smart." The makings of a powerful school culture are in there somewhere.

Bill and Melinda Gates share the belief that all kids can achieve and that the school culture makes the difference. That's why, in addition to extensive investments in better health care for Third World children, their foundation has donated millions of dollars to alter the culture of large American high schools by restructuring them into smaller learning units (schools-within-a-school) and providing specialized training for teachers. It seems to be working. I'm not surprised. Are you?

I'm most familiar with the results from three Gates Foundation award recipients in St. Paul, Minnesota: Harding High School, Highland Park High School, and Johnson High School. After just five years of collaboration with the Bill & Melinda Gates Foundation, the results are in:

- The four-year graduation rates increased up to 19 percent in the three schools.
- The graduation rates for Black students grew even more significantly, thus narrowing a troublesome achievement gap between majority and minority students.
- The percentage of students going on to higher education in the three schools exceeded the overall St. Paul percentage.
- Test scores showed significant gains among Blacks and low-income students.

As Kay Arndt, principal at Johnson, explains, "The project allowed our school to restructure itself into small learning communities that helped teachers and school leaders do a better job of reaching out to kids and meeting their needs."

Obviously, Kay Arndt thinks that culture can make a big difference in achievement levels. So do Bill and Melinda Gates. I wouldn't argue with the richest man in the world. Would you?

Even more impressive than the St. Paul experience are the results from the Downtown College Prep School in San José, California. DCP, as the school is affectionately known, is a charter school intentionally designed to create a culture of achievement for a group of students that some schools—maybe even your school—might give up on. The DCP student population is made up almost entirely of low-income, minority students (mostly Hispanic).

From its inception, Greg Lippman and Jennifer Andaluz, the two young teachers who founded the school, made an astonishing promise to any parents willing to enroll their children. They guaranteed that all students would be qualified for a four-year college or university upon graduation.

And then they set out to establish a school culture that would deliver on this promise. In order to move all students from the "dropout slide to the college track," the founders built their culture around their simple, no-nonsense mission (e.g., no lofty, vague buzzwords—just prepare all kids for college) and a few key core values, including:

- "Ganas" (motivation, the will to succeed, true grit)
- Seriousness (an academic culture that encourages all students to be serious about their schoolwork)
- An ethos of honesty (admit and face problems realistically)
- Persistence (stay on task, allow no student to drift)
- Accountability
- Personalization
- Relentless cheerfulness (a sense of humor and a willingness to laugh at problems)

Not surprisingly, the entire school program, from the small size, which permits adults to notice problems quickly, to the daily tutorial period (90 minutes of work with no talking) was then organized to translate the vision and values into action.

By the time the first class reached graduation, the scoreboard lit up with positive results:

- On the challenging California Standards Tests, DCP students surpassed the state average in biology, and 67 percent tested as proficient or advanced in U.S. history.
- DCP students also exceeded the state average on the California Academic Performance Index (API) compared to all high schools with similar demographics.
- DCP had the second-highest pass rate on the State Graduation Exam in the entire San José district.
- DCP ranked third among all San José high schools, even though it had the highest number of students not fluent in English (90 percent) and tied for first in the number of low-income pupils.

and

- ALL GRADUATES WERE ACCEPTED FOR COLLEGE!

Lippman and Andaluz gambled on a culture of achievement for underachievers—and won. Of course, the real winners were the DCP students and parents. For more information about the DCP experience, read Joanne Jacobs's popular book, *Our School* (2005).

On a much broader scale, I know an entire community that has tried to redefine its culture to boost student achievement and help young people survive and thrive in all areas of life. In the 1990s, my hometown became a self-proclaimed "Children First" community.

Led by a partnership of city government, public schools, health care providers, the faith community, and local business leaders, the initiative issued a call to all residents of all ages to become asset builders for youth. The idea was that everyone (institutions and individuals alike) can support and bolster the community's children and youth. Remember—it takes a whole village . . . well, you know how that goes.

The emphasis was on an attitude rather than on any specific program or set of activities. Each person was challenged to find their own way to help the community put its children first. Whether it was a simple smile from a neighbor, a scholarship donated by an anonymous adult, a civic club volunteering to read to elementary school students, or business leaders serving as afterschool homework helpers in a low-income housing complex, it all counted.

Naturally, the effort paid off, or I wouldn't have included it in this book. The nationally recognized Search Institute has conducted a multi-year, longitudinal study of developmental assets in sixth to twelfth graders in the community. The research covered 40 internal and external assets ranging from supportive neighborhoods, parental involvement, and caring school environments to participation in sports, religious involvement, and an optimistic view of the future.

The study's findings concluded that the overall level of assets experienced by young people rose significantly across the board each year, while at-risk behaviors (e.g., drugs, crime, and other antisocial behavior) have decreased.

Why is this important? Because the more developmental assets students possess, the fewer negative behaviors they exhibit and the better they do in school and in life. It's a simple success formula that works every time. And it continues to work.

Interestingly, every elementary and secondary school in my hometown has been recognized by the federal government as a National School of Excellence, the high school has been identified as one of the top 500 high schools in the nation by *Newsweek* magazine, the 2006 State Teacher of the Year teaches in the local Spanish Immersion School, and the community has been chosen as one of the top 100 communities in the country for youth by the America's Promise organization, founded by former U.S. secretary of state Colin Powell. Coincidence? Accident? Fluke? Unlikely!

Whether it is in three public high schools in St. Paul, a charter school in California, or my suburban community, a positive school culture can boost achievement dramatically.

Still doubtful? Skeptical? Unconvinced? There are countless more examples, studies, and statistics that support the powerful link between school culture and pupil achievement. During the 1970s and 1980s, repeated research showed that culture is a primary contributor to academic achievement. But you don't need research findings—just look at your own school. Which classrooms have the most healthy, cohesive, positive, supportive, and affirming classroom climates? Now, which have the largest achievement gains year in and year out? Voilà! They're the same, aren't they? I rest my case.

The key questions for school leaders should be:

- What factors in a positive school culture up the odds in favor of high achievement for all pupils?
- How do I build them into my school environment?

The answers may surprise some administrators, teachers, and parents. It's not strict discipline and constant pressure that make a difference. The two characteristics of a healthy culture that most directly drive peak performances are love and relationships.

Of course, I'm not talking about romantic love or the scandalous kind of love some teachers have for students of the opposite sex that we read about in the headlines. What works in effective school cultures is "tough love" that allows adults to give kids what they really need, not just what's easy, fun, or what the kids (and their parents) think they want or need.

It is a sense of genuine affection built on mutual respect. It is unconditional love that accepts people as they are, finds what's right in each person, sees what the other person can become, and never gives up.

This form of love is a rare commodity in many offices, assembly lines, cubicles, and, unfortunately, in some classrooms; but it shouldn't be. Love is what it takes for more productivity, higher profits—or higher test scores.

All the great teachers love pupils this way; but not every pseudoteacher with a degree and a certificate does. Some don't even like their own students. Hire teachers who are genuinely passionate about kids (in a nonpsychopathic way) and you have taken the huge, first step toward a full-blown, results-oriented environment.

The second big-ticket item in the culture that drives achievement is related to the first. It's simply the nature of the relationships within the organization. Powerful personal relationships can affect motivation, commitment, persistence, and resilience.

A good school never fails; it just runs out of time.

—Author unknown

Deep and intentional relationships help create the conditions for all children to learn and succeed in school.

—Hank Rubin, writer

Strong relationships require informal time spent together and repeated opportunities to know each other in different (unpressured, non-competitive) situations. As principal or superintendent, you can create these opportunities by arranging social events, service projects, group learning experiences, creative activities, travel opportunities, and visioning exercises.

Obviously, this all requires extra work. That's why the best culture builders spend as much time working on the relationships within the organization as they do working on the budget of the organization.

Other cultural components that boost student achievement include:

- *High Standards.* Meeting mediocre standards is still mediocre achievement. Low standards are an insult. High standards are a vote of confidence.

- *High Expectations.* It's true that you tend to get what you expect. If you don't believe in self-fulfilling prophecies, you've never watched a master teacher at work. There can be no achievement where there is no expectation of success.

- *Freedom to Risk, Fail, and Risk Again.* Where there is no prospect for a second chance, some students won't risk taking the first chance.

- *Incentives and Rewards.* Business leaders have always known that what gets rewarded gets done. It's that way in schools too. But in education, the rewards aren't necessarily monetary, or even tangible. The culture's most powerful rewards and incentives are peer recognition and approval. If the school and the community value sports enough, it produces championships. Just think what happens when these cultures value academic achievement that much. In the best schools, effort itself is recognized as a legitimate form of achievement.

- *Appreciation of Differences.* No two people learn exactly alike, so all students shouldn't be taught exactly alike. Results-oriented cultures celebrate differences and address diversity to help everyone achieve.

- *Realism.* Achievement requires a willingness to admit problems and face them up front. It's better to celebrate mistakes than to suppress them.

- *Valuing Education, Schooling, and Intelligence.* In a culture of achievement, being smart and getting good grades aren't nerdy. Being smart is an advantage, and working smart is a necessity.

- *Mutual Support.* In the best cultures, helping each other is just the way people do business every day, and it's not limited to adults helping kids. It applies to kids helping kids and adults helping adults as well. Everyone needs help to achieve. It's stupid not to get and offer all the help you can.

- *Rigorous Work Ethic.* When the culture believes that hard work pays off, students work hard and achieve more. That doesn't mean "all work and no play." Fun is also a core value in all successful schools.
- *A Sense of Humor and Playfulness.* When the organization encourages a little self-deprecating humor, students and teachers are more likely to take risks. Learning can be fun if you let it. Let it.

Researchers have found a connection between a well-developed sense of humor and problem solving.

—Dyan Machan, career counselor and writer

These are the basic ingredients for promoting achievement within the culture. That makes these the areas to work on if you want to get better results.

As leader of the school, you can't handcraft the school's culture; but you can't ignore it either. All things suffer from neglect.

There's a better reason for working to create a positive culture than simply because it feels good and makes going to work more fun. It also provides better outcomes. After all, schools have bottom lines, too.

Unfortunately, there are two schools of thought among educators regarding results. Some are willing to settle for the perception of success (faux results and the appearance of improvement). They are willing to manipulate data, inflate grades, dumb down the curriculum, switch tests to compare themselves to more favorable norm groups, and—in some cases—falsify information to create the illusion of results.

Smoke and mirrors aren't just for magicians. School administrators can be illusionists, too. One humorist has even suggested, with tongue in cheek, using a Grade Change Form to help manufacture better results (see example).

Actually, contriving to produce phony results is more work than actually producing good results. Besides, fabricating or fudging on results is a bad idea, because you'll be found out, people will get mad, you'll lose your job, and children suffer in the process. It's better to produce real results through actual achievement. A positive school culture will do that for you.

By now, I hope all the doubters have become convinced that the culture of the organization makes the difference between student success and only so-so achievement or possible failure. If this weren't true, Bill Gates wouldn't be spending millions to improve the learning culture in schools. And I wouldn't go to the trouble of writing an entire book on the subject. And you wouldn't read it if I did.

Culture works. If yours works for students, staff, parents, and community members, you will have the best possible results-oriented work environment. If you do this and nothing else, you will go down in history as a true hero of the organization.

The trick is to make the concept of culture understandable and meaningful for all participants. Sound complicated? Maybe. But like most subjects, culture building can be broken down to fairly simple terms. You'll find the simplified version in Chapter 12.

Universal Grade Change Form

Name of school _____

To: Mr./Mrs./Ms. _____ From: _____

I think my grade in your course/class _____should be changed from
_____ to _____ for the following reason(s):

_____ 1. The person whose paper I copied made a better grade than I did.

_____ 2. I'm on a sports team and my tutor couldn't find a copy of your exam.

_____ 3. I was unable to do well because of the following illness:
    ___ Mono
    ___ Acute alcoholism
    ___ STDs
    ___ Broken baby finger
    ___ Pregnancy
    ___ Fatherhood

_____ 4. This course was:
    ___ Too early. I was not awake.
    ___ At lunchtime. I was hungry.
    ___ Too late. I was tired.

_____ 5. My (dog, cat, gerbil) (ate, wet on, threw up on) my (book, notes, paper) for this course.

_____ 6. I don't have a reason, I just want a better grade.

SOURCE: Adapted from *Tidbits of Lake Minnetonka,* March 22, 2005.

12

No Deposit, No Return

Culture Building Made Simple

One of my favorite sayings I got off a soda bottle: "NO DEPOSIT, NO RETURN." To me that means you'll get out of life about what you are willing to put in.

—John Nabor, four-time Olympic
Gold Medal swimmer

If you are not in the habit of reading the quotes at the beginning of each chapter, take time and do it now. What the quotation above says about life applies to the school's culture as well.

In fact, the culture of the school is a big part of your life, and you pretty much get out of the culture what you put into it. It's an investment. It's a "no deposit, no return" kind of deal.

As principal or superintendent, you can choose to do nothing and just let the character of the school become what it will be—for good or ill. Or you can use your position, power, prestige, authority, and influence as head of the school to coax, nudge, negotiate, and steer the culture in the direction of your vision. It's a definitive choice.

If you see yourself as a manager just trying to get the job done and make it through each day until you can hang it up and go fishing, you'll probably opt to let the culture drift and take care of itself. Contrarily, if you view yourself as a leader who wants to make a difference and leave a lasting legacy, you won't be able to leave the culture alone. You'll choose to take a shot at moving the culture of the organization closer to your dream of what the school can become.

The second choice is, by far, the most difficult and challenging, but also the most fun.

Of course, having read this far, you know that culture building is a complex, nuanced, layered, creative process. Don't let that scare you off. In addressing all the details, angles, possibilities, and choices in creating a positive and healthy school environment, a book like this may make it seem more daunting and overwhelming than it really is.

Don't get caught up in overthinking or overanalyzing the dynamics involved. It is possible to strip culture building down to the bare essentials. What's left is a highly manageable task—not easy, but manageable.

Basically, creating a culture that works for everyone just means defining the shared values that you want the school to stand for, and then living the values—walking the talk. That's it. There isn't any more.

It all starts with the mission—what the school says it is. Every educational institution has a mission statement. In some, it is just a bunch of words—mostly glittering generalities—strung together, which don't have much direct bearing on what goes on in the organization on a daily basis. In a real school, however, the mission is the engine that drives all major choices, decisions, and actions and tells the staff what's going right and what's not.

As the legendary former CEO of General Electric, Jack Welch, explains, "The mission answers the question, 'How do we intend to win?'" A good mission statement signals what's important, defines what constitutes success, balances direction with inspiration, and guides the allocation of resources.

Obviously this is important stuff; but crafting a mission is the easy part. It's after you have a well-defined mission that the real work begins. Mission making is made easier by the fact that we all basically know and agree on what's true, right, and beautiful. We just need to write it down. That's why most mission statements look alike.

Once the mission is agreed upon, however, the challenge is to keep it front and center. As Memphis superintendent Carol Johnson has admonished, "We have to keep the main thing the main thing." That's why some school leaders take creative measures to keep the mission fresh in everyone's mind.

We've all heard of administrators who post the mission statement prominently throughout the school or have it printed on laminated, wallet-size cards to give to everyone in the organization; but how about placing a penny in your shoe so that every time you feel the coin during the day, you're reminded of the mission; or mixing a copy of the mission, beliefs, and goals in with the bills in your wallet so that every time you pull out a bill, you see them as well? These schemes have worked for some of your counterparts.

Such gimmicks may seem a little far-fetched. The important point is that a mission statement isn't a true mission unless people are aware of it and think about it as they go through their daily activities. If a gimmick helps, good leaders aren't above using it to get the job done.

A strong culture isn't built merely by remembering or thinking about the school's mission statement. Words or thoughts may make promises; but only action can deliver. It's the modeling of the mission that makes all the difference in culture building.

By the end of the day, the culture of any organization isn't formed by the words in the mission statement or laminated list of beliefs or core values, but by the actions of its leaders and other key players. In schools, teachers and other staff members are always watching the behavior of administrators, looking for clues as to what the "real" culture is, behind the words and between the lines.

As an example, I remember an incident when an irate patron burst into my office insisting that a swimming pool supervisor in one of our community education centers be fired immediately. He blustered, shook his fist, and did his best to be menacing and intimidating.

Shaking with rage, the angry visitor alleged that the employee had been drinking on the job and holding sexual trysts in her office when she should have been supervising young swimmers—obviously, very serious charges.

Almost shouting in my face now, he demanded that the employee be terminated on the spot. I asked for proof. He said "everyone" knew it was happening. I asked for proof. He said he had evidence. I asked to see it.

He ignored my request and played his trump card. He threatened to take his story to Channel 5, a local TV station, if I didn't agree to sever the supervisor right now.

My reply was, "Go ahead. I don't give a s—t about Channel 5! I only care about the truth." I made it clear that if he or anyone else provided evidence of misconduct, we would act. If he didn't have any proof, we would investigate on our own anyway. If his allegations were true, the supervisor would be dealt with; but I would not fire or discipline any employee solely on the basis of rumor, gossip, innuendo, half-truths, or unsubstantiated allegations.

I refused to be bullied and told him to leave my office and not return—with or without Channel 5—until he was willing to share whatever evidence he had.

My visitor stalked out, still fuming. I never saw him again. I never learned what his real problem was; but no evidence surfaced or was discovered. The employee kept her job and was not disciplined.

Word got around about the incident (including the epithet about Channel 5). It helped strengthen a bond of mutual respect and trust within the organization. It became one of the stories that perpetuate and reinforce the culture.

Leaders can't always defend employee behavior. But they can always be fair and refuse to be stampeded into premature judgment or action. This is modeling the values; and this is a sign of a healthy culture.

The truth is that whenever you see a long-term, successful school, nonprofit agency, or other organization, you will usually find a culture in which the leaders live by the mission and core values. Despite headline-grabbing horror stories of duplicity and deceit to the contrary, it's even true in businesses.

Fred Zimmerman, retired St. Thomas University professor, uses the farm implement behemoth John Deere & Company as an example in his book *The Turnaround Experience* (McGraw-Hill, 1991). Zimmerman explains the company's long-standing history of phenomenal success this way:

> Quality, innovation, integrity and commitment have been the core values of John Deere and Company since founder John Deere articulated them in the mid-nineteenth century.
>
> Too important to be relegated to mere plaques or printed documents, the values were reinforced by Deere's everyday behavior.
>
> Reinforcing values by behavior is harder, of course. It takes little effort to whip up mission, values and vision statements. It is much more time-consuming and expensive to live those missions. . . .
>
> Living values creates meaningful involvement. Publicizing values often is synthetic window dressing.

According to Zimmerman, the leadership at John Deere has consistently modeled the mission by insisting on quality, operating with integrity, and keeping commitments.

That's what should happen in every business. That's what should happen in every school. In my school. And in yours. It's the old "practice what you preach" advice. It's still the secret to successful culture building.

I'm intrigued by the fact that the United States government has spent $50 million developing "gait recognition technology." Since everyone's gait is unique (like fingerprints), it is now possible to tell who you are by how you walk.

What an amazing metaphor for creating a school environment. You see, it's by the way you walk the talk (or don't) that people can tell what kind of leader you are and what kind of school culture will evolve under your leadership.

Can culture building be made simple? Sure. (Note that there's a difference between "simple" and "easy.") When you strip away all the bells and whistles, all that's left is the nuts and bolts—just say what you believe, and then act that way. It's that simple.

Simple or not, we seem to be doing something wrong in the nation's schools. Too many kids are hurt and hurting. Too many are not learning, not achieving, and not even trying. Too many excited, eager-to-learn kinder-gartners become sullen, sad, scornful, antischool, and antisocial teenagers in just 13 short years. Too much creativity is lost. Too much talent is wasted. Too many canaries stop singing altogether.

But we can change all that. You can change part of it yourself. You can foster a school culture in which all students find their voices—and their songs—and keep on singing.

When all the canaries learn to sing, the school is filled with what famed author William Saroyan calls "canary cheerfulness." Alene Christiano would like that.

Resource A

FAQs

Frequently Asked Questions

A prudent question is one-half of wisdom.

—Francis Bacon
English philosopher, essayist, and statesman

No one really becomes a fool until he stops asking questions.

—Charles P. Steinmetz
scientist and inventor

———————————— ❦ ————————————

Every effective culture allows questions, welcomes questions, encourages questions, and uses questions to increase understanding and generate discussion. So a chapter with a question-and-answer format is a natural fit for this book.

Following are some of the most frequently asked questions about school culture that can be answered with some brevity, clarity, and specificity. In each case, I've given my best answer. (If you know a better one, feel free to substitute it.)

• **What is the best time to initiate a change in the culture of the school?**

If there is a serious problem, the best time to start is now. If there is no particular sense of urgency, it is often expeditious to time a new initiative to correspond with a natural break or new beginning (e.g., the arrival of a new leader,

(Continued)

(Continued)

a new term, or the introduction of a new reorganization plan) when people are anticipating a fresh start anyway.

- **How long does it take to turn around a school culture?**

Most experts agree that a full-blown, 180-degree turnaround can take three to five years. This includes completely internalizing and institutionalizing a whole new set of values, expectations, norms, rules, and roles—and a new definition of success.

Things can start getting better as soon as tomorrow morning. Significant improvement can happen rather quickly, even though a total transformation may stretch out over years.

- **If leadership is "removing obstacles," what is the most important obstacle to remove first? (Where do you start?)**

Start by removing any semblance of a self-deprecating attitude of inadequate expectations. The greatest obstacle to success usually isn't lack of money. Or inadequate staffing. Or subpar facilities. It's a mentality of mediocrity.

Too many school cultures operate under limited visions and self-imposed ceilings. It never occurs to many teachers and administrators that their school can become truly great. Until they think it can, it can't.

The best school leaders redefine the horizon and help colleagues believe that anything is possible. In the award-winning movie *Toy Story,* the character Buzz Lightyear talks about reaching "infinity and beyond." More principals and superintendents should think like Buzz Lightyear. Not thinking big enough is the single greatest impediment to achieving a winning culture.

By the way, the second biggest obstacle is bureaucracy. Removing bureaucratic barriers gives teachers time to teach. Better yet, it can provide them time to actually think. Wouldn't that be a revolutionary concept?

- **What is the most important ingredient (prerequisite) for a positive school culture?**

Passion for kids. The second most important element is passion for teaching. The third is passion for public education. Passion trumps all other cultural components. It is a secret weapon. Without it, you can't win.

Without passion, the culture of the organization is lifeless, listless, and lackluster. It is mostly words. With passion, the culture becomes real life.

Where does the passion come from? From passionate people. Hang on to the ones you have. And add as many more as possible. It's a key to building a winning culture.

- **What is the single most important thing a school leader can do to guarantee a positive school culture now and in the future?**

Hire the right people. There isn't anything in your job description more important than staffing. Every new employee you bring onboard is potentially a 30-year asset—or a million-dollar mistake.

Cultures are of the people, by the people, and for the people. (Abe Lincoln couldn't have said it better.) If you hire champions, you're well on your way to a championship. If you hire second-rate people, don't expect a first-rate school culture. It's not going to happen.

- **What kinds of teachers are needed for a strong school culture?**

All kinds—as long as they care about kids and are passionate about their teaching. If all teachers on the staff—no matter how strong they are—are too much alike, the culture can quickly become inbred and insipid. Diversity is the strength of all enduring school cultures.

Of course, we all have an image of the true master teacher. Here are the qualities I wish all teachers possessed:

- *Wisdom.* The knowledge of what can be taught and what must be taught
- *Intuition.* A sense of the sensitivities of those they teach
- *Boldness.* The courage to be a "propagandist for truth"
- *Eloquence.* The ability to speak, not only to a sea of faces but also directly to the heart of a student
- *Flair.* A style that is different and refreshing—a unique "batting stance" in the classroom
- *Presence.* The quality that existentialists call "Dasien"—a state of "being there" with the student—of looking at the world from inside the skin of a youngster

If all teachers were like this, an optimum learning environment would be a given. Lacking perfection, I'll settle for teachers who care deeply—and show it.

- **Is culture building expensive? Should it have its own budget?**

Some functions related to culture building do require expenditures (e.g., staff development and strategic planning), but these are expenditures that all schools incur.

The good news is that the basic building blocks of a culture that works for everyone are cost-free, including:

Personal attention	Rigorous standards
Accountability	Commitment to excellence
Meaningful dialogue	Choices
Caring environment	Second chances
Listening	Sense of humor
Honest feedback	Dedication

(Continued)

(Continued)

Hope	Challenging assignments
High expectations	Seriousness of purpose
Excitement about learning	Firm, fair discipline
Straight talk	Pride in accomplishment
Authentic teaching	Dignity

One of the well-kept secrets of school leadership is that the things that make a truly great school culture are not big-ticket items. What matters most costs the least. That pretty much eliminates the primary excuse for not trying to improve the school environment.

- **How can a new administrator find out or figure out who are the real informal leaders and power brokers within the culture?**

Never assume that the people with the titles are the real opinion makers, trendsetters, and power sources in the organization. Ask your predecessors for their assessment. They can afford to be objective. Also observe whom people look to or listen to when problems or questions arise. If necessary, conduct a simple four-step Cultural Power Analysis:

1. Ask those in leadership positions (those with titles) to list three people they think are most powerful and influential within the culture.

2. In turn, ask the people listed by the positional leaders to list the three people they think are the most powerful and influential people within the culture.

3. Repeat the process with all those people listed as a result of Step 2.

4. Analyze all the results. The people whose names appear most frequently on all the lists should be the unofficial leaders within the culture. This isn't a perfect instrument, but it is usually a reliable measure.

Once you have identified the informal leaders, keep them in the loop, ask their advice, and use their influence to influence others. It's another secret of successful culture building.

- **Has the No Child Left Behind (NCLB) legislation had a positive or negative impact on school cultures?**

Both. For some struggling schools, the legislation has provided a much-needed focus and rallying point.

For other schools, NCLB has created frustration and dissent as teachers feel limited and locked in to teaching for tests; and some schools get a bad rap by being penalized for silly circumstances, such as the absence of a few minorities or special education students on test day.

I've known high schools included among the top 500 high schools in the country by national publications, which were also cited for not making "adequate yearly progress" by NCLB standards. What's wrong with this picture?

For schools with the very best cultures, however, NCLB is irrelevant. They have already moved far beyond the minimum performance levels and accountability measures prescribed in the legislation and operate on much broader and higher levels of educating children.

- **Do labor unions have a positive or negative effect on the school culture?**

Again, the answer is both. Teachers' unions share many goals with the overall school culture and can help reinforce many core values. Unions can also drive a wedge between the teaching staff and the administration by fostering an "us-versus-them" mentality.

That's why it is important to develop a relationship with union leaders based on trust and mutual respect. The way to do this is to avoid dirty tricks, downplay excess emotion, remain reasonable and respectful, tell the truth, honor confidences, and keep your word—every time and all the time.

- **What is the effect of a teacher strike on the school culture?**

It can be devastating. No one wins in a strike; and it sometimes takes years for the school to "heal" in the aftermath.

I've seen a few real-life examples firsthand. My wife was once involved in a teacher strike where one of her friends, who couldn't in good conscience support the work stoppage, crossed the picket line. When the strike was over, the friend was never again fully accepted or forgiven by the other teachers. Strikers have long memories.

Likewise, some years ago, I was part of a situation in which teachers refused to teach summer school—except for the drivers' training instructors, who felt obligated to their students and worked anyway. Up until the time they retired, the regular teachers involved remained estranged from the drivers' education staff.

Strikes always leave scars. That's why putting the school culture back together after a strike is a lot like starting over. It requires time and patience. It helps speed the healing, however, if school leaders have treated strikers with respect and dignity and kept the lines of communication open throughout the rift.

(Continued)

(Continued)

- **Can a school culture change directions in midstream?**

You bet. Even God allows U-turns. Only a toxic culture refuses to budge or alter course. Healthy cultures make midcourse corrections all the time to adjust or adapt to new developments.

The trick is to make changes that are consistent with core values and principles and to change deliberately, consciously, intentionally, and intelligently. Flip-flopping in response to fickle popular opinion—or to chase the latest flavor of the month—doesn't count.

It's okay to change directions as long as the school is moving in a positive direction. One thing never changes—putting children first!

- **Do students still fail in a positive school culture?**

I'm afraid so. No culture is foolproof. The best culture can only give every student every chance to succeed.

Some will still choose to fail. A winning school culture never runs out of second chances and never gives up on any child.

- **Can the school culture be independent of the culture of the community?**

Not entirely. And you shouldn't want it to be independent or separate from the community. For better or worse, the cultures of the school and the community are interactive. They shape and change each other.

Schools, including yours, can be only as strong, creative, and progressive as the community allows.

- **Can a school culture be beyond repair?**

Maybe not. But some are so far gone that it's probably easier to start over.

Some schools, particularly in inner cities and poor rural areas, have become so mired down in a culture of defeat and despair that hope is a forgotten commodity. People just go through the motions. No one cares much anymore.

For these schools, the best answer may be to dismantle the organization, redefine attendance boundaries, create a new school with a different student body, and bring in fresh teachers, fresh ideas, and fresh energy. That's what charter schools do. Some of them have given students and families a new lease on life and learning.

- **How do you know when you're done?**

This is a trick question. You never finish creating the best school culture possible. The character of the school—any school—is in a constant state of flux: evolving, emerging, and transforming.

People come and go. Even the people who stay don't stay the same. They grow, mature, and learn. Conditions change. Circumstances fluctuate. Context alters. You never step into the same culture twice.

I can think of at least three schools that once rose to national prominence on the basis of their creative and innovative cultures. They became models. Received nationwide publicity. Attracted visitors from around the globe. The schools raked in huge sums of grant money. And their principals wrote books that became bestsellers.

Now, not so many years later, they are largely forgotten and operate in relative obscurity. What happened?

They've lost their edge. They stopped innovating. They thought they were done.

A school's culture is a process, not a product. The fun is in the doing, not in getting done. The best you can hope for is to foster a school culture that accepts change, welcomes change, adjusts to change, shapes change, and keeps on changing.

Obviously, this section could go on and on. Questions are a renewable resource. The more questions that are asked, the more questions that arise. Nevertheless, these are all the questions that time and space will allow for now.

However, if you have questions on what worries people most about culture building, see the following section.

Resource B

FSWs

Frequently Stated Worries

One of the wisest men in Des Moines tells me that he has kept track of the 50 principal things he's worried about in the last ten years, jotting 'em down at the bottom of the pages in his diary in green ink. He finds that not one of these actually happened; but they bothered him just as much as if they had.

—Harlen Miller, writer

"Life's too short to worry."
"Yes, that's what worries me."

—Author unknown

———————— ✀ ————————

As far as I know, Kathleen Kimball-Baker was the first person to include an "FSWs" section in a book (*Tag, You're It!* published by Search Institute in 2003). It's a useful addition because some readers don't have questions; but they do have worries, fears, apprehensions, concerns, misgivings, and reservations.

As long as administrators are worrying, they're stalled. Once their worries are addressed, allayed, or alleviated, they are free to move on. To alter Franklin Roosevelt's classic admonition, "The only thing we have to worry about is worry itself."

Following are some of the most common worries I've heard expressed about building a positive school culture—along with some of my reactions, suggestions, and recommendations. Take them for what they're worth.

- **I worry that I'm not good enough, smart enough, brave enough, strong enough, or charismatic enough to shape the culture of an entire organization.**

If you worry about whether or not you are good enough for the job, you probably are good enough for the job. Intelligence, strength, bravery, and charisma are not prerequisites for culture building. Passion and commitment are.

Besides, you won't be shaping a positive school culture all by yourself. Culture building is a team sport. You don't have to do all the heavy lifting. Your primary responsibilities are to assemble the right team, help define the mission, remove obstacles, cheerlead, and watch good things happen.

- **I worry that I'm too young (or too old) to be taken seriously as a culture builder.**

This should be the least of your worries. Passion has no age requirements. If you care enough and are serious about building a culture that works for everyone, you'll be taken seriously.

The worst thing you can do is to adopt a false persona (e.g., trying to act older or younger than you really are). The best thing you can do is to be yourself (act your age) and let your true emotions and commitment show through. Authenticity is always taken seriously, and passion transcends all ages.

- **I worry that the factions in our school will never agree on shared values.**

This is wasted worry. Educators, of all stripes, are more alike than different. School factions seldom disagree on ends, although they may be polar opposites on means.

After all, what legitimate faction opposes (at least out loud) better teaching, accountability, fiscal fitness, parental involvement, community partnerships, or lifelong learning? These are baseline values shared by all segments of the staff.

Build on the areas of common agreement that make up the foundation of every healthy school culture and the secondary areas of disagreement will fall into perspective.

- **I worry that our school is too big.**

If your enrollment is more than 1,000 pupils, you have cause for concern. Large size is no friend of an affirming, empowering culture.

It's difficult to create a culture that works for everyone in a large institution. Difficult—but not impossible. Even some of the nation's largest corporations have done it (e.g., GE, Southwest Airlines, Home Depot, and John Deere). No matter how large your school is, you can do it too.

The trick is to minimize bureaucracy, maximize human interaction, and break down the organization into smaller, more personal, and more manageable units.

In 1961, I helped open a new high school organized around a "little school" (schools-within-a-school) concept. The idea was to capture the benefits of both a large and a small school. There were only a half dozen such schools in the entire nation. Many people thought it was much ado about nothing.

Today, however, megaschools in every major city in the country are seeking ways to create smaller learning units, and Bill Gates is spending millions of dollars to help them. I won't say I told you so. Oops, I already did.

- **I worry that the bottom 15 percent of the staff won't buy into the culture.**

Don't worry. The bottom feeders of the organization are not essential to successful culture building. If you had to wait for universal acceptance, any attempt to change the environment would be dead in the water.

Your time is best spent working with the top trendsetters, the movers and shakers, and the critical middle. You don't need everyone onboard all the time. You just need a critical mass moving together in the same direction.

That momentum will drag the stragglers and naysayers along kicking and screaming into the future—or at least render them irrelevant.

- **I worry about a few abrasive teachers who don't want to comply with the rules, insist on pushing the envelope, and challenge the mores of the school culture.**

Don't sweat it. A strong culture can accommodate a few mavericks. In fact, they keep the culture honest.

If a teacher is good with kids, I can put up with a modicum of abrasiveness. Can't you?

- **I worry that budget cutting will stymie efforts to improve the school's culture.**

Fortunately, culture building is not a budget item that can be cut. (See "Is culture building expensive?" in Resource A, page 135.)

In fact, a strong culture can make budget cutting easier and less painful; and sometimes, budget cutting can even strengthen the existing culture. (There is something to this "misery loves company" notion after all.)

(Continued)

(Continued)

For example, like some of you, I was once part of a protracted budget reduction process caused by drastic enrollment decline. Sadly, the reductions included extensive teacher layoffs.

As it turned out, many teachers were placed on unrequested leave for several years in a row and, each time, managed to return for another year as the result of attrition and retirements.

Because of the nature of the existing culture, extensive efforts were made to humanize the reduction process and to assist terminated teachers in finding other jobs, in and out of public education.

In most cases, the affected personnel accepted the realities of the situation, without blaming school leaders unduly. A sense of humor helped.

At the time, state rules required that each teacher involved be served with a personally delivered notice of termination (education's equivalent of business's infamous "pink slip"). For some teachers, it became an annual ritual. I remember playfully chasing one teacher all around the building each year to serve the dreaded notice. It wasn't a funny circumstance, but we had as much fun with it as we could. Sometimes, it's better to laugh than to cry.

Years later, I am still friends with many teachers whom I laid off repeatedly during darker times. The point is that a healthy culture transcends budget problems—even staff reductions.

- **I worry that adversarial relationships at the bargaining table will carry over and interfere with my efforts to build a better school culture.**

It's tricky playing the dual roles of negotiator and culture builder at the same time. But it can be done. Of course, just hoping that it will all work out isn't good enough. It takes conscious effort and intentional problem solving. I know. I've done it both ways.

At one time, I was chief bargainer for the district during negotiations over a new contract with the clerical union. It was a contentious process. Pay equity was a highly charged emotional issue during that period—and the clerks believed that custodial union members received better pay and benefits for jobs of comparable worth. They were probably right.

At the bargaining table, I thought I had to be hard-nosed. Away from the table, I tried to be a servant boss and remove obstacles to a better culture for everyone—including clerical personnel.

It wasn't working. Relationships became increasingly strained. Eventually, both sides engaged in a little trash talk. The union's newsletter even described me as "tacky." Although the contract was eventually settled, the adversarial feeling of mistrust persisted and carried over into the everyday workplace.

I finally decided to make a concerted and conscious effort to improve relationships with the clerical union representatives. I made it one of my job targets and worked on it for a year.

I went to special lengths to keep the union leaders informed about what was going on and what was coming up. I shared full budget information with them. I took more time explaining the district's positions and rationale. Then I listened—and listened—and tried to empathize with their positions.

Strangely enough, I was as surprised as anyone when it actually worked. At the end of the year, my wife and I were invited as special guests to the union's annual banquet. A first!

From then on, I was able to maintain an open relationship with the union leadership that enabled us to resolve many issues without resorting to formal grievances or testy mediation or arbitration hearings.

Collective bargaining seems to be a necessary evil in today's schools; but it doesn't have to delay or derail culture building. Unless you let it.

- **I worry about what gangs will do to the school culture.**

Worry won't help; but gangs are a legitimate source of concern. Fortunately, many schools have had success neutralizing gang presence by banning weapons, gang colors, gang insignias, and gang signs on school property. Even gang members appreciate a break and a safe haven now and then.

Gangs can be only as strong as the school and the community allow them to be. It is possible to create a productive culture of hope, even in a gang-infested neighborhood.

- **I worry that a skeptical local media will sabotage efforts to change the school's culture.**

The media must be part of a culture that works for everyone. It's your job to woo 'em, wow 'em, and win 'em over.

Of course, you'll never gain media support by being combative. My old mentor, Carl Holmstrom, taught me to "never argue with someone who buys ink by the barrel." It never pays to be argumentative, defensive, or whiny.

The way to get the media on your side is to be honest, be accessible, be yourself—and produce results.

Regardless of their bias, all media representatives value "good education." You share this value with them. Start there. Show how the proposed changes in school culture will translate into better learning and higher achievement, and the media will soon become your school's best friend.

- **I worry that voters will reject a proposed levy referendum and what that will do to the culture of the school.**

If the community turns down the school's appeal for money, the voters haven't done anything wrong. The school has.

(Continued)

(Continued)

For some reason, the culture of the school isn't working for the community, and the community isn't buying into the school's goals. It's a wake-up call.

One rejection is only a bump in the road, not the end of the road. It merely means you have more work to do.

Start by finding out the real reasons for the "No" vote. Obviously, something—community perceptions, school aspirations, or communication between the two—has to change. The time to start making the needed changes is now.

- **I worry that culture building takes too much time.**

Culture building is a time-consuming job; but it is only a job. I hope you work to live and do not live to work. You will have more fresh energy for culture building if you live a balanced life.

Leave the school and its culture at school. You may have to bring home some work some nights; but you don't have to bring the school culture home every night.

Take a tip from the native Hawaiian people who practice *Ho'-ponopono,* which means to "make right." Each evening they close their eyes and practice the gentle art of "letting go" of everything from the day. Try it. You'll be a better culture builder if you do.

- **I worry because I don't always know what I'm doing.**

Welcome to the club. Culture building isn't like applying a formula or following a recipe. It's pioneering, pathfinding, and breaking new ground. A culture isn't constructed from prefabricated parts. It's invented as you go along.

That's why good culture builders possess a high degree of "ambiguity tolerance"—the ability to live with unsolved problems and uncharted courses. By definition, culture building is a perpetual state of partial fulfillment.

So you don't have to know in advance exactly what to do every step along the way or have all the answers. Don't worry. If you stick to the mission and live the values, you will be all right.

Obviously, there is a lot a person can choose to worry about in building a positive school environment; but worry won't help. In fact, worry is the wasteland of leadership. Don't worry about it.

Resource C

What Others Say About Organizational Culture

Culture isn't just one aspect of the game—it is the game.

> —Louis V. Gerstner, former CEO
> of IBM, author of *Who Says
> Elephants Can't Dance?* (2003)

Our motto is culture before curriculum.

> —Greg Lippman, cofounder
> DCP Charter School, San José, CA

The boundaries of culture and rainfall never follow survey lines.

> —J. Frank Dobie, writer

Nothing is more important about a school than its culture.

> —Roland S. Barth
> educational author and consultant

Everywhere men are recognizing that organizations should have souls.

> —Alva Konkle, writer

Individuals come and go—but organizations preserve knowledge, behaviors, mental images, norms, and values over time and translate these cultural expectations to newcomers. It is the culture that keeps the organization going beyond the tenure of any single leader.

> —Author unknown

Every successful school leader knows that culture is everything.

—Laraine Roberts, California
School Leadership Academy

Even with schools with weak or threadbare cultures, it is usually possible to find something worth celebrating. These stories, values, traditions, heroes, and heroines provide a vital starting point for updating, reinvigorating and reframing the school's identity and culture.

—Leo G. Bolman, University of
Missouri at Kansas City

Pain can induce a united, cohesive culture.

—Barbara Ehrenreich, author

Create a culture of creativity to better position your company for success.

—Pat Fallon, ad agency founder

Culture shapes people, but cultures are changeable.

—David Brooks
New York Times columnist

Schools are refuges of integrity and fair play.

—Gerald W. Bracey
educational researcher

Culture—that is, the values and assumptions that shape its members—is all the marines have. It is what holds them together.

—Thomas Ricks, author of
Making the Corps (1998)

Our curriculum is better because of our commitment to build positive connections with all students before anything else. We focus on building constructive relationships with students and providing educational experiences for them that they will treasure for years to come.

—Scott Gengler, principal
Watertown-Mayer High
School, Watertown, MN

Schools are the most germ-filled workplaces. . . . Research shows that phones, desks and keyboards used by teachers harbor up to 20 times more bacteria than those in other workplaces. It's not that surprising, because teachers' clients are kids—a germ's best friend.

—Charles Gerbo, professor of environmental
microbiology, University of Arizona, as quoted
in *USA Today,* June 4, 2006.

Our culture is our competitive edge.

—Mike Smith, CEO, Lands' End

Culture isn't the property of the leaders and the powerful.

—Mary Pipher, author of
The Middle of Everywhere (2003)

Historical lore and contemporary stories form the anchor and spirit of school culture.

—T. K. Deal and K. Peterson
educator-authors

Everyone who works in a school is not only entitled to a unique and personal vision of the way he or she would like the school to become, but has an obligation to uncover, discover, and rediscover what that vision is and contribute to the betterment of the school community.

—Roland S. Barth
educational author and consultant

What a great teacher, a great parent, a great psychotherapist, and a great coach have in common is a deep belief in the potential of the person with whom they are concerned.

—Nathaniel Branden
psychologist

. . . no job seekers (from the corporate world) I ever met expressed nostalgia for the camaraderie of the workplace—probably there wasn't any.

—Barbara Ehrenreich
author

An effective school has a positive school culture.

—L. A. Bartel
educator-author

The values of friendship, risk, trust, fun, and love are the hallmarks of a successful team-based organization.

—John R. Hoyle
leadership specialist
Texas A&M University

Quality schoolwork . . . can only be achieved in a warm, supportive classroom environment. It cannot exist in an adversarial relationship. . . . After all, there must be trust. . . . Without trust, neither students nor teachers will make the effort needed for quality work.

—William Glasser, founder
William Glasser Institute

We do not make a world of our own, but fall into institutions already made, and have to accommodate ourselves to them to be useful at all.

—Ralph Waldo Emerson
writer and philosopher

Dairy farmers have the "Got Milk" campaign to promote the dairy industry. But the federal government, instead of getting behind schools and promoting them, it's punishing them. Sending the message to the public that schools are no good is bad public policy. It makes the argument that the school is falling apart and the education system is to blame.

—A Minnesota parent and education
official reporting on the No Child
Left Behind legislation

Culture is omnipresent. It is underneath and behind all that goes on in the life of the school.

—R. Bruce Williams, education
consultant and group facilitator

Who the hell would want a lousy job like that? Long hours, low pay and what gratitude do you get for dealing with their brats?

—Frank McCourt, Pulitzer Prize–winning
author and New York City
teacher for 20 years

A school's culture and the classroom climate are the direct results of attitudes, behaviors, and interactions among teachers, administrators, parents, students, and staff.

—Author unknown

The culture of the organization makes clear what the organization stands for—its values, its beliefs, its true self (as distinguished from its publicly stated goals).

—Robert C. Owens
educator-author

Culture is the glue that holds the elements of the school together.

—Jeffrey Glanz, from *What Every
Principal Should Know About
Cultural Leadership* (2006)

Resource D

Related Readings

Alvesson, Mats. (2002). *Understanding Organizational Culture.* Stockholm, Sweden: Lund University.

Bakke, Dennis W. (2005). *Joy at Work: A Revolutionary Approach to Fun on the Job.* Seattle, WA: PVG.

Beaudoin, Marie-Nathalie & Taylor, Maureen. (2004). *Creating a Positive School Culture.* Thousand Oaks, CA: Corwin Press.

Bridges, William. (2000). *The Character of Organizations: Using Personality Type in Organization Development.* Palo Alto, CA: Davies-Black Publishing.

Cooperrider, David & Whitney, Diana. (2005). *A Positive Revolution in Change.* San Francisco: Berrett-Koehler Publishers.

Deal, Terrence & Peterson, Kent D. (1999). *Shaping School Culture: The Heart of Leadership.* San Francisco: Jossey-Bass.

Driskill, Gerald W. & Brenton, Angela Lairol. (2005). *Organizational Culture in Action: A Cultural Analysis Workbook.* Little Rock: University of Arkansas Press.

Gerstener, Louis V. (2003). *Who Says Elephants Can't Dance?: Leading a Great Enterprise Through Dramatic Change.* New York: Collins.

Giancola, Joseph M. & Hutchison, Janice K. (2005). *Transforming the Culture of School Leadership.* Thousand Oaks, CA: Corwin Press.

Glanz, Jeffrey. (2006). *What Every Principal Should Know About Cultural Leadership.* Thousand Oaks, CA: Corwin Press.

Jacobs, Joanne. (2005). *Our School: The Inspiring Story of Two Teachers, One Big Idea, and the School That Beat the Odds.* New York: Palgrave Macmillan.

Reagan, Timothy C., Case, Charles W., & Brubacher, John W. (2000). *Becoming a Reflective Educator: How to Build a Culture of Inquiry in the School.* Thousand Oaks, CA: Corwin Press.

Rubin, Hank. (2002). *Collaborative Leadership: Developing Effective Partnerships in Communities and Schools.* Thousand Oaks, CA: Corwin Press.

Williams, R. Bruce. (2006). *36 Tools for Building Spirit in Learning Communities.* Thousand Oaks, CA: Corwin Press.

Index

CORWIN PRESS

The Corwin Press logo—a raven striding across an open book—represents the union of courage and learning. Corwin Press is committed to improving education for all learners by publishing books and other professional development resources for those serving the field of PreK–12 education. By providing practical, hands-on materials, Corwin Press continues to carry out the promise of its motto: **"Helping Educators Do Their Work Better."**

NATIONAL ASSOCIATION OF SECONDARY SCHOOL PRINCIPALS

Promoting Excellence in School Leadership

The National Association of Secondary School Principals—promoting excellence in school leadership since 1916—provides its members the professional resources to serve as visionary leaders. NASSP further promotes student leadership development through its sponsorship of the National Honor Society®, the National Junior Honor Society®, and the National Association of Student Councils®. For more information, visit www.principals.org.